KAREN ARMSTRONG is the author of *A History of God* and *The Spiral Staircase*, among other bestsellers. She is among the world's most foremost commentators on religion, and an important advocate for interfaith understanding.

Visit www.AuthorTracker.co.uk for exclusive information on your favourite HarperCollins authors.

The Great Transformation: The World in the Time of Buddha, Socrates, Confucius and Jeremiah

A Short History of Myth

The Spiral Staircase: A Memoir

The Battle for God: Fundamentalism in Judaism, Christianity and Islam

A History of God: The 4,000-Year Quest of Judaism, Christianity and Islam

In the Beginning: A New Interpretation of Genesis

Muhammad: A Biography of the Prophet

Islam: A Short History

Buddha: A Biography

Through the Narrow Gate: A Memoir of Convent Life

History of Jerusalem: One City, Three Faiths

Holy War: The Crusades and Their Impact on Today's World

Visions of God: Four Medieval Mystics and Their Writings

The Gospel According to Woman: Christianity's Creation of the Sex War in the West

MUHAMMAD

Prophet for Our Time

KAREN ARMSTRONG

ATLAS BOOKS

HARPER PERENNIAL
London, New York, Toronto and Sydney

Harper Perennial
An imprint of HarperCollins*Publishers*
77–85 Fulham Palace Road
Hammersmith
London w6 8jb

isbn-13 978-0-00-723248-2
isbn-10 0-00-723248-9

Set in PostScript Adobe Caslon with Ariel,
Galliard and Optima display

Printed and bound in Great Britain by Clays Ltd, St Ives plc

For Sally Cockburn

Contents

Introduction 13

Chapter One: Mecca 21

Chapter Two: Jahiliyyah 53

Chapter Three: Hijrah 89

Chapter Four: Jihad 125

Chapter Five: Salam 165

Glossary 215

Notes 231

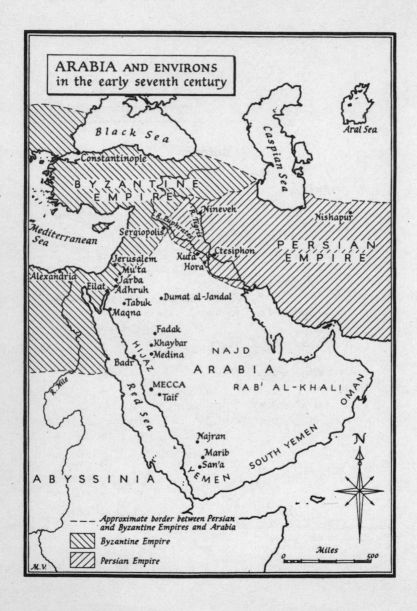

ARABIA AND ENVIRONS
in the early seventh century

Black Sea

Constantinople

BYZANTINE
EMPIRE

Mediterranean
Sea

Caspian Sea

Aral Sea

Nineveh

Nishapur

R. Euphrates

R. Tigris

Sergiopolis

Ctesiphon

PERSIAN
EMPIRE

Jerusalem

Kufa

Mu'ta

Hora

Jarba

Alexandria

Adhruh

Eilat

Tabuk

Dumat al-Jandal

Maqna

Fadak

Khaybar

HIJAZ

Medina

NAJD

Badr

ARABIA

R. Nile

MECCA

RAB' AL-KHALI

OMAN

Taif

Red Sea

Najran

Marib

San'a

SOUTH YEMEN

ABYSSINIA

YEMEN

N

– – – Approximate border between Persian
        and Byzantine Empires and Arabia

Byzantine Empire

Persian Empire

M.V.

Miles

0   500

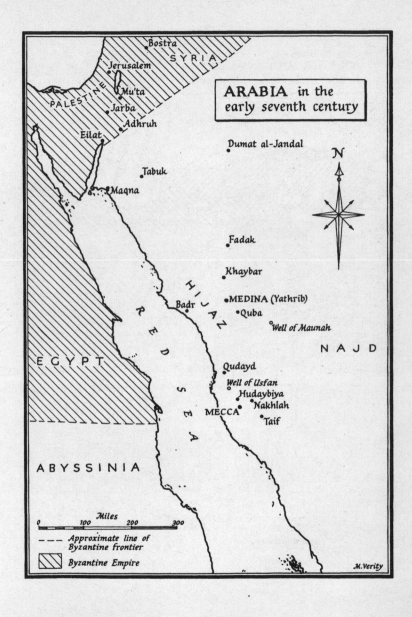

Bostra

Jerusalem

SYRIA

Mu'ta

PALESTINE

Jarba

Adhruh

Eilat

ARABIA in the
early seventh century

Dumat al-Jandal

Tabuk

Maqna

N

Fadak

Khaybar

RED SEA

HIJAZ

Badr

MEDINA (Yathrib)

Quba

Well of Maunah

NAJD

EGYPT

Qudayd

Well of Usfan

Hudaybiya

Nakhlah

MECCA

Taif

ABYSSINIA

Miles

0   100   200   300

Approximate line of
Byzantine frontier

Byzantine Empire

M. Verity

Introduction

THE HISTORY OF A RELIGIOUS tradition is a continuous dialogue between a transcendent reality and current events in the mundane sphere. The faithful scrutinize the sacred past, looking for lessons that speak directly to the conditions of their lives. Most religions have a figurehead, an individual who expresses the ideals of the faith in human form. In contemplating the serenity of the Buddha, Buddhists see the supreme reality of Nirvana to which each of them aspires; in Jesus, Christians glimpse the divine presence as a force for goodness and compassion in the world. These paradigmatic personalities shed light on the often dark conditions in which most of us seek salvation in our flawed world. They tell us what a human being can be.

Muslims have always understood this. Their scripture, the Qur'an, gave them a mission: to create a just and decent society, in which all members were treated with respect. The political well-being of the Muslim community was, and is, a matter of supreme importance. Like any religious ideal, it is almost insuperably difficult to fulfill, but after each failure, Muslims have tried to get up and begin again. Many Islamic rituals, philosophies, doctrines, sacred texts, and shrines are the result of frequently anguished and self-critical contemplation of the political events of Islamic society.

The life of the Prophet Muhammad (c. 570–632 CE) was as crucial to the unfolding Islamic ideal as it is today. His career revealed the inscrutable God's activity in the world, and illustrated the perfect surrender (in Arabic, the word for "surrender" is *islam*) that every human being should make to the divine. Beginning during the Prophet's lifetime, Muslims had to strive to understand the meaning of his life and apply it to their own. A little more than a hundred years after Muhammad's death, as Islam continued to spread to new territories and gain converts, Muslim scholars began to compile the great collections of Muhammad's sayings (*ahadith*) and customary practice (*sunnah*), which would form the basis of Muslim law. The sunnah taught Muslims to imitate the way Muhammad spoke, ate, loved, washed, and worshipped, so that in the smallest details of their daily existence, they reproduced his life on earth in the hope that they would acquire his internal disposition of total surrender to God.

At about the same time, in the eighth and ninth centuries, the first Muslim historians began to write about the life of the Prophet Muhammad: Muhammad ibn Ishaq (d. 767); Muhammad ibn 'Umar al-Waqidi (d. c. 820); Muhammad ibn Sa'd (d. 845); and Abu Jarir at-Tabari (d. 923). These historians were not simply relying on their own memories and impressions, but were attempting a serious historical reconstruction. They included earlier documents in their narratives, traced oral traditions back to their original source, and, though they revered Muhammad as a man of God, they were not entirely uncritical. Largely as a result of their efforts, we know more about Muhammad than about nearly any other founder of a major religious tradition. These early sources are indispensable to any biographer of the Prophet, and I will frequently refer to them in these pages.

The work of Muhammad's first biographers would probably not satisfy a modern historian. They were men of their time and often included stories of a miraculous and legendary nature that we would interpret differently today. But they were aware of the complexity of their material. They did not promote one theory or interpretation of events at the expense of others. Sometimes they put two quite different versions of an incident side by side, and gave equal weight to each account, so that readers could make up their own minds. They did not always agree with the traditions they included, but were trying to tell the story of their Prophet as honestly and truthfully as they could. There are lacunae in their accounts. We know practically nothing about Muhammad's early life before he began to receive what he believed were revelations from God at the age of forty. Inevitably, pious legends developed about Muhammad's birth, childhood, and youth, but these clearly have symbolic rather than historical value.

There is also very little material about Muhammad's early

political career in Mecca. At that time, he was a relatively obscure figure, and nobody thought it worthwhile to make note of his activities. Our main source of information is the scripture that he brought to the Arabs. For some twenty-three years, from about 610 to his death in 632, Muhammad claimed that he was the recipient of direct messages from God, which were collected into the text that became known as the Qur'an. It does not contain a straightforward account of Muhammad's life, of course, but came to the Prophet piecemeal, line by line, verse by verse, chapter by chapter. Sometimes the revelations dealt with a particular situation in Mecca or Medina. In the Qur'an, God answered Muhammad's critics; he reviewed their arguments; he explained the deeper significance of a battle or a conflict within the community. As each new set of verses was revealed to Muhammad, the Muslims learned it by heart, and those who were literate wrote it down. The first official compilation of the Qur'an was made in about 650, twenty years after Muhammad's death, and achieved canonical status.

The Qur'an is the holy word of God, and its authority remains absolute. But Muslims know that it is not always easy to interpret. Its laws were designed for a small community, but a century after their Prophet's death, Muslims ruled a vast empire, stretching from the Himalayas to the Pyrenees. Their circumstances were entirely different from those of the Prophet and the first Muslims, and Islam had to change and adapt. The first essays in Muslim history were written to address current perplexities. How could Muslims apply the Prophet's insights and practice to their own times? When the early biographers told the story of his life, they tried to explain some of the passages in the Qur'an by reproducing the historical context in which these particular revelations had come down to Muhammad. By understanding what had prompted a particular Qur'anic teaching, they could relate it to their own situation by means of a disciplined process of analogy. The historians and thinkers of the time believed that learning about the Prophet's struggles to make the word of God audible in the seventh century would help them to preserve his spirit in their own. From the very start, writing about the Prophet Muhammad was never a wholly antiquarian pursuit. The process continues today. Some Muslim fundamentalists have based their militant ideology on the life of Muhammad; Muslim extremists believe that he would have condoned and admired their atrocities. Other Muslims are appalled by these claims, and point to the extraordinary pluralism of the Qur'an, which condemns aggression and sees all rightly guided religions as deriving from the one God. We have a long history of Islamophobia in Western culture that dates back to the time of the Crusades. In the twelfth century, Christian monks in Europe insisted that Islam was a violent religion of the sword, and that Muhammad was a charlatan who imposed his religion on a reluctant world by force of arms; they called him a lecher and a sexual pervert. This distorted version of the Prophet's life became one of the received ideas of the West, and Western people have always found it difficult to see Muhammad in a more objective light. Since the destruction of the World Trade Center on September 11, 2001, members of the Christian Right in the United States and some sectors of the Western media have continued this tradition of hostility, claiming that Muhammad was irredeemably addicted to war. Some have gone so far as to claim that he was a terrorist and a pedophile.

We can no longer afford to indulge this type of bigotry, because it is a gift to extremists who can use such statements to "prove" that the Western world is indeed engaged on a new crusade against the Islamic world. Muhammad was not a man of violence. We must approach his life in a balanced way, in order to appreciate his considerable achievements. To cultivate an inaccurate prejudice damages the tolerance, liberality, and compassion that are supposed to characterize Western culture.

I became convinced of this fifteen years ago, after the fatwah of Ayatollah Khomeini had sentenced Salman Rushdie and his publishers to death because of what was perceived to be a blasphemous portrait of Muhammad in *The Satanic Verses*. I abhorred the fatwah and believed that Rushdie had a right to publish whatever he chose, but I was disturbed by the way some of Rushdie's liberal supporters segued from a denunciation of the fatwah to an out-and-out condemnation of Islam itself that bore no relation to the facts. It seemed wrong to defend a liberal principle by reviving a medieval prejudice. We appeared to have learned nothing from the tragedy of the 1930s, when this type of bigotry made it possible for Hitler to kill six million Jews. But I realized that many Western people had no opportunity to revise their impression of Muhammad, so I decided to write a popular accessible account of his life to challenge this entrenched view. The result was *Muhammad: A Biography of the Prophet,* which was first published in 1991. But in the wake of September 11, we need to focus on other aspects of Muhammad's life. So this is a completely new and entirely different book, which, I hope, will speak more directly to the terrifying realities of our post–September 11 world.

As a paradigmatic personality, Muhammad has important lessons, not only for Muslims, but also for Western people. His life was a jihad: as we shall see, this word does not mean "holy war," it means "struggle." Muhammad literally sweated with the effort to bring peace to war-torn Arabia, and we need people who are prepared to do this today. His life was a tireless campaign against greed, injustice, and arrogance. He realized that Arabia was at a turning point and that the old way of thinking would no longer suffice, so he wore himself out in the creative effort to evolve an entirely new solution. We entered another era of history on September 11, and must strive with equal intensity to develop a different outlook.

Strangely, events that took place in seventh-century Arabia have much to teach us about the events of our time and their underlying significance—far more, in fact, than the facile sound bites of politicians. Muhammad was not trying to impose religious orthodoxy— he was not much interested in metaphysics—but to change people's hearts and minds. He called the prevailing spirit of his time *jahiliyyah.* Muslims usually understand this to mean the "Time of Ignorance," that is, the pre-Islamic period in Arabia. But, as recent research shows, Muhammad used the term jahiliyyah to refer not to an historical era but to a state of mind that caused violence and terror in seventh-century Arabia. Jahiliyyah, I would argue, is also much in evidence in the West today as well as in the Muslim world.

Paradoxically, Muhammad became a timeless personality because he was so rooted in his own period. We cannot understand his achievement unless we appreciate what he was up against. In order to see what he can contribute to our own predicament, we must enter the tragic world that made him a prophet nearly fourteen hundred years ago, on a lonely mountain top just outside the holy city of Mecca.

Chapter One

Mecca

Afterwards he found it almost impossible to describe the experience that sent him running in anguish down the rocky hillside to his wife. It seemed to him that a devastating presence had burst into the cave where he was sleeping and gripped him in an overpowering embrace, squeezing all the breath from his body. In his terror, Muhammad could only think that he was being attacked by a *jinni*, one of the fiery spirits who haunted the Arabian steppes and frequently lured travellers from the right path. The jinn also inspired the bards and soothsayers of Arabia. One poet described his poetic vocation as a violent assault: his personal jinni had appeared to him without any warning, thrown him to the ground and forced the verses from his mouth.[1] So, when Muhammad heard the curt command "Recite!" he immediately assumed that he too had become possessed. "I am no poet," he pleaded. But his assailant simply crushed him again, until—just when he thought he could bear it no more—he heard the first words of a new Arabic scripture pouring, as if unbidden, from his lips.

He had this vision during the month of Ramadan, 610 CE. Later Muhammad would call it *layla al-qadr* (the "Night of Destiny") because it had made him the messenger of Allah, the high god of Arabia. But at the time, he did not understand what was happening. He was forty years old, a family man, and a respected merchant in Mecca, a thriving commercial city in the Hijaz. Like most Arabs of the time, he was familiar with the stories of Noah, Lot, Abraham, Moses, and Jesus and knew that some people expected the imminent arrival of an Arab prophet, but it never occurred to him that *he* would be entrusted with this mission. Indeed, when he escaped from the cave and ran headlong down the slopes of Mount Hira', he was filled with despair. How could Allah have allowed him to become possessed? The jinn were capricious; they were notoriously unreliable because they delighted in leading people astray. The situation in Mecca was serious. His tribe did not need the dangerous guidance of a jinni. They needed the direct intervention of Allah, who had always been a distant figure in the past, and who, many believed, was identical with the God worshipped by Jews and Christians.*

Mecca had achieved astonishing success. The city was now an international trading center and its merchants and financiers had become rich beyond their wildest dreams. Only a few generations earlier, their ancestors had been living a desperate, penurious life in

---

*In Arabic, the word *Allah* simply means "God."

the intractable deserts of northern Arabia. Their triumph was extraordinary, since most Arabs were not city dwellers but nomads. The terrain was so barren that people could only survive there by roaming ceaselessly from place to place in search of water and grazing land. There were a few agricultural colonies on the higher ground, such as Ta'if, which supplied Mecca with most of its food, and Yathrib, some 250 miles to the north. But elsewhere farming—and, therefore, settled life—was impossible in the steppes, so the nomads scratched out a meagre existence by herding sheep and goats, and breeding horses and camels, living in close-knit tribal groups. Nomadic (*badawah*) life was a grim, relentless struggle, because there were too many people competing for too few resources. Always hungry, perpetually on the brink of starvation, the Bedouin fought endless battles with other tribes for water, pastureland, and grazing rights.

Consequently the *ghazu* (acquisition raid) was essential to the badawah economy. In times of scarcity, tribesmen would regularly invade the territory of their neighbors in the hope of carrying off camels, cattle, or slaves, taking great care to avoid killing anybody, since this could lead to a vendetta. Nobody considered this in any way reprehensible. The ghazu was an accepted fact of life; it was not inspired by political or personal hatred, but was a kind of national sport, conducted with skill and panache according to clearly defined rules. It was a necessity, a rough-and-ready way of redistributing wealth in a region where there was simply not enough to go around.

Even though the people of Mecca had left the nomadic life

behind, they still regarded the Bedouin as the guardians of authentic Arab culture. As a child, Muhammad had been sent to live in the desert with the tribe of his wet nurse in order to be educated in the badawah ethos. It made a profound impression on him. The Bedouin were not very interested in conventional religion. They had no hope of an afterlife and little confidence in their gods, who seemed unable to make any impact on their difficult environment. The tribe, not a deity, was the supreme value, and each member had to subordinate his or her personal needs and desires to the well-being of the group, and fight to the death, if necessary, to ensure its survival. Arabs had little time for speculation about the supernatural but were focused on *this* world. Fantasy was useless in the steppes; they needed pragmatic, sober realism. But they had evolved a chivalric code, which, by giving meaning to their lives and preventing them from succumbing to despair in these harsh conditions, performed the essential function of religion. They called it *muruwah*, a complex term that is difficult to translate succinctly. Muruwah meant courage, patience, endurance; it consisted of a dedicated determination to avenge any wrong done to the group, to protect its weaker members, and defy its enemies. To preserve the honor of the tribe, each member had to be ready to leap to the defense of his kinsmen at a moment's notice and to obey his chief without question.

Above all, a tribesman had to be generous and share his livestock and food. Life in the steppes would be impossible if people selfishly hoarded their wealth while others went hungry. A tribe that was rich today could easily become destitute tomorrow. If you had been miserly in good days, who would help you in your hour of need? Muruwah made a virtue out of this necessity, encouraging the *karim* (the "generous hero") to care little for material goods so that he would not become depressed by his life of deprivation. A truly noble Bedouin would take no heed for the morrow, showing by his lavish gifts and hospitality that he valued his fellow tribesmen more than his possessions. He had to be prepared to give all his wealth—his camels, flocks, and slaves—to others, and could squander his entire fortune in a single night by putting on a superb feast for his friends and allies. But the generosity of the karim could be self-destructive and egotistic: He could reduce his family to poverty overnight, simply to demonstrate the nobility that flowed in his veins and enhance his status and reputation.

Muruwah was an inspiring ideal, but by the end of the sixth century, its weaknesses were becoming tragically apparent. Tribal solidarity (*'asibiyyah*) encouraged bravery and selflessness, but only within the context of the tribe. There was no concept of universal human rights. A Bedouin felt responsible merely for his blood relatives and confederates. He had no concern for outsiders, whom he regarded as worthless and expendable. If he had to kill them to benefit his own people, he felt no moral anguish and wasted no time in philosophical abstractions or ethical considerations. Since the tribe was the most sacred value, he backed it, right or wrong. "I am of Ghazziyya," sang one of the poets. "If she be in error, I will be in error; and if Ghazziyya be guided right, I will go with her."[2] Or, in the words of a popular maxim: "Help your brother whether he is being wronged or wronging others."[3]

Each tribe had its own special brand of muruwah, which, the Arabs believed, had been inherited from the founding fathers of the tribe and was passed, like other physical and mental characteristics, from one generation to another. They called this tribal glory *hasab* ("ancestral honor").[4] As the source of their particular genius, tribesmen revered their forefathers as the supreme authority and this inevitably encouraged a deep and entrenched conservatism. The way of life (sunnah) that the ancients had bequeathed to their descendants was sacred and inviolable. "He belongs to a tribe whose fathers have laid down for them a sunnah," another poet explained, "Every folk has its own traditional sunnah; every folk has its objects of imitation."[5] Any deviation—however trivial—from ancestral custom was a great evil. A practice was approved not because of its inherent decency or nobility, but simply because it had been sanctioned long ago by the fathers of the tribe.

The Bedouin could not afford to experiment. It would be criminally irresponsible to ignore the *shari'ah*, the path to the waterhole that had been the lifeline of your people from time immemorial. You learned to survive by following a set of rules whose value had been proven by experience. But this unquestioning acceptance of tradition could lead to rampant chauvinism: the sunnah of your people was the best and you could contemplate no other way of doing things. You could only preserve the honor of your tribe by refusing to bow to any other authority, human or divine. A karim was expected to be proud, self-regarding, self-reliant, and aggressively independent. Arrogance was not a fault but a sign of nobility, whereas humility showed that you came from defective stock and had no aristocratic blood in your veins. A base-born person was genetically destined to be a slave (*'abd*); that was all he was good for. A true karim could not submit to anybody at all. "We refuse to all men submission to their leading," sang one poet, "till we lead them ourselves, yea without reins!"[6] A karim would maintain this defiant self-sufficiency even in the presence of a god, because no deity could be superior to a truly noble human being.

In the steppes, the tribe needed men who refused to be bowed by circumstance and who had the confidence to pit themselves against overwhelming odds. But this haughty self-reliance *(istighna')* could easily become reckless and excessive. The Bedouin was easily moved to extremes at the smallest provocation.[7] Because of his exalted sense of honor, he tended to respond violently to any perceived threat or slight. He did not simply act in self-defense; true courage lay in the preemptive strike. It is not enough for "a warrior, fierce as a lion, to strike back and chastise the enemy who has struck him with a blow," cried the poet Zuhayr ibn 'Abi Salma, "he should rather attack first and become an aggressor when no one wrongs him."[8] The courage praised by the tribal poets was an irresistible impulse that could not and should not be restrained. If a wrong was done to a single member of his tribe, a karim felt the duty of vengeance as a physical pain and a tormenting thirst.[9] It was a tragic worldview. The Bedouin tried to glorify their struggle, but their life was grim and there was no hope of anything better. All beings, they believed, came under the sway of *dahr* ("time" or "fate"), which inflicted all manner of suffering on humanity; a man's life was determined in advance. All things passed away; even the successful warrior would die and be forgotten. There was an inherent futility in this life of ceaseless struggle. The only remedy against despair was a life of pleasure—especially the oblivion of wine.

In the past, many of the Bedouin had tried to escape from the steppes and build a more secure, settled (*hadarah*) life, but these attempts were usually frustrated by the scarcity of water and arable land, and the frequency of drought.[10] A tribe could not establish a viable settlement unless it had either accumulated a surplus of wealth—an almost impossible feat—or took over an oasis, as the tribe of Thaqif had done in Ta'if. The other alternative was to become an intermediary between two or more of the rich civilizations in the region. The tribe of Ghassan, for example, which wintered on the border of the Byzantine empire, had become clients of the Greeks, converted to Christianity, and formed a buffer state to defend Byzantium against Persia. But during the sixth century, a new opportunity arose as a result of a transport revolution. The Bedouin had invented a saddle that enabled camels to carry far heavier loads than before, and merchants from India, East Africa, Yemen, and Bahrain began to replace their donkey carts with camels, which could survive for days without water and were ideally suited to navigate the desert. So instead of avoiding Arabia, foreign merchants trading in luxury goods—incense, spices, ivory, cereals, pearls, wood, fabrics, and medicines—began to take their caravans by the more direct route to Byzantium and Syria through the steppes, and employed the Bedouin to guard their merchandise, drive the camels, and guide them from one well to another.

Mecca became a station for these northbound caravans. It was conveniently located in the center of the Hijaz, and even though it was built on solid rock, which made agriculture impossible there, settlement was feasible because of an underground water source that the Arabs called Zamzam. The discovery of this seemingly miraculous spring in such an arid region had probably made the site holy to the Bedouin long before the development of a city in Mecca. It attracted pilgrims from all over Arabia, and the Kabah, a cube-shaped granite building of considerable antiquity, may originally have housed the sacred utensils of the Zamzam cult. During the fifth and sixth centuries, the spring and the sanctuary (*haram*) were controlled by a succession of different nomadic tribes: Jurham, Khuza'ah, and finally in the early sixth century by the Quraysh, Muhammad's tribe, who drove out their predecessors and were the first to construct permanent buildings around the Kabah.

The founding father of the Quraysh was Qusayy ibn Kilab, who had brought together a number of previously warring clans that were loosely related by blood and marriage and formed this new tribe, just as Mecca was becoming a popular center for long-distance trade. The name "Quraysh" may have been derived from *taqarrush* ("accumulation" or "gaining").[11] Unlike the Jurham and Khuza'ah, who had not been able to abandon badawah, they acquired a capital surplus that made a settled lifestyle possible. First they managed to secure a monopoly of the north-south trade, so that they alone were allowed to service the foreign caravans. They were also able to control the mercantile activity within Arabia that had been stimulated by the influx of international commerce. During the first part of the sixth century, Bedouin tribes had begun to exchange goods with one another.[12] Merchants congregated in a series of regular markets that were held each year in different parts of Arabia, and were so arranged that traders circled the peninsula in a clockwise direction. The first market (*suq*) of the year was held in Bahrain, the most densely populated region; the next were held successively in Oman, Hadramat, and Yemen, and the cycle concluded with five consecutive suqs in and around Mecca. The last fair of the year was held in 'Ukaz immediately before the month of the *hajj*, the traditional pilgrimage to Mecca and the Kabah.

During the first half of the sixth century, the Quraysh had started to send their own caravans to Syria and Yemen, and gradually they established themselves as independent traders. But despite this success, they knew that they were vulnerable. Because agriculture was impossible in Mecca, they relied entirely on the exchange of commodities, so if the economy failed, they would starve to death. Everybody, therefore, was involved in commerce, as bankers, financiers, or merchants. In the agricultural settlements, the badawah spirit remained virtually intact because it was more compatible with farming, but the Quraysh were forced to cultivate a strictly commercial ethos that took them away from many of the traditional values of muruwah. They had, for example, to become men of peace, because the kind of warfare that was endemic in the steppes would make business impossible. Mecca had to be a place where merchants from any tribe could gather freely without fear of attack. So the Quraysh steadfastly refused on principle to engage in tribal warfare and maintained a position of aloof neutrality. Before their arrival, there had often been bloody battles around Zamzam and the Kabah, as rival tribes tried to gain control of these prestigious sites. Now, with consummate skill, the Quraysh established the Haram, a zone with a twenty-mile radius, with the Kabah at its center, where all violence was forbidden.[13] They made special agreements with Bedouin tribes, who promised not to attack the caravans during the season of the trade fairs; in return these Bedouin confederates were compensated for the loss of income by being permitted to act as guides and protectors of the merchants.

Trade and religion were thus inextricably combined in Mecca. The pilgrimage to Mecca was the climax of the suq cycle, and the Quraysh reconstructed the cult and architecture of the sanctuary so that it became a spiritual center for all the Arab tribes. Even though the Bedouin were not much interested in the gods, each tribe had its own presiding deity, usually represented by a stone effigy. The Quraysh collected the totems of the tribes that belonged to their confederacy and installed them in the Haram so that the tribesmen could only worship their patronal deities when they visited Mecca. The sanctity of the Kabah was thus essential to the success and survival of the Quraysh, and their competitors understood this. In order to attract pilgrims and business away from the Quraysh, the governor of Abyssinia and Yemen constructed a rival sanctuary in Sana'a. Then, in 547, he led an army to Mecca to prove that the city was not, after all, immune from warfare. But, it was said, his war elephant fell upon its knees when it reached the outskirts of Mecca, and refused to attack the Haram. Impressed by this miracle, the Abyssinians returned home. The Year of the Elephant became a symbol of Mecca's sacred inviolability.[14]

But the cult was not simply an empty, cynical exploitation of piety. The rituals of the hajj also gave the Arab pilgrims a profound experience. As they converged on Mecca at the end of the suq cycle, there was a sense of achievement and excitement. The caravans were checked by the Quraysh, their camels relieved of their burdens, and, after paying a modest fee, the merchants and their servants were free to pay their respects to the Haram. As they made their way through the narrow streets of the suburbs, they uttered ritual cries, announcing their presence to the gods who were awaiting their arrival. After their long trek around the peninsula, this reunion with the sacred symbols of their tribes felt like a homecoming. When they reached the Kabah, surrounded by the 360 tribal totems, they began to perform the traditional rites in Mecca and its environs, which may originally have been devised to bring on the winter rains. They jogged seven times between the hills of Safa and Marwah, to the east of the Kabah; ran in a body to the hollow of Muzdalifah, the home of the thunder god; made an all-night vigil on the plain beside Mount 'Arafat, sixteen miles outside the city; hurled pebbles at three pillars in the valley of Mina; and finally, at the end of their pilgrimage, sacrificed their most valuable female camels, symbols of their wealth and—hence—of themselves.

The most famous ritual of the hajj was the *tawaf*, seven circum-ambulations of the Kabah in a clockwise direction, a stylized re-enactment of the circular trade route round Arabia, which gave the Arabs' mercantile activities a spiritual dimension. The tawaf became a popular devotional exercise, and citizens and their guests would perform it all the year round. The structure of the Haram acquired an archetypal significance, which has been found in the shrines of other cities in the ancient world.[15] The Kabah, with its four corners representing the four cardinal directions, symbolized the world. Em-bedded in its eastern wall was the Black Stone, a piece of basalt of meteoric origin, which had once fallen brilliantly from the sky, link-ing heaven and earth. As the pilgrims jogged around the huge gran-ite cube, following the course of the sun around the earth, they put themselves in harmony with the fundamental order of the cosmos. The circle is a common symbol of totality, and the practice of cir-cumambulation, where you constantly come back to your starting point, induces a sense of periodicity and regularity. By circling round and round the Kabah, pilgrims learned to find their true orientation and their interior center; the steady rhythm of the jog gradually emp-tied their minds of peripheral thoughts and helped them to enter a more meditative state.

The reformed rites made Mecca the center of Arabia. Where other pilgrims had to leave their homelands and journey to remote sites, the Arabs had no need to leave the peninsula, which remained a law unto itself. All this reinforced the centrality of Mecca as the focus of the Arab world.[16] The city was also isolated and this gave the Arabs a rare freedom. Neither Persia nor Byzantium, the great powers of the region, had any interest in the difficult terrain of Arabia, so the Quraysh could create a modern economy without imperial control. The world passed through Mecca, but did not stay long enough to interfere. Arabs were able to develop their own ideology and could interpret the knowledge and expertise of their more sophisticated neighbors as they chose. They were not pressured to convert to an alien religion or conform to official orthodoxy. The closed circle of both the trade cycle and the hajj rituals symbolized their proud self-sufficiency, which, as the years passed, would become a mark of their urban culture.

Their separation from the great powers meant that the Meccan economy was not damaged by their decline in fortune; indeed, the Quraysh were able to profit from it. By 570, the year of Muhammad's birth, Persia and Byzantium were locked in a debilitating series of wars with one another that would fatally weaken both empires. Syria and Mesopotamia became a battleground, many of the trade routes were abandoned, and Mecca took control of all the intermediary trade between north and south.[17] The Quraysh had become even more powerful, yet some were beginning to feel that they were paying too high a price for their success. As the sixth century drew to a close, the city was in the grip of a spiritual and moral crisis.

The old communal spirit had been torn apart by the market economy, which depended upon ruthless competition, greed, and individual enterprise. Families now vied with one another for wealth and prestige. The less successful clans* felt that they were being pushed to the wall. Instead of sharing their wealth generously, people were hoarding their money and building private fortunes. They not only ignored the plight of the poorer members of the tribe, but exploited the rights of orphans and widows, absorbing their inheritance into their own estates. The prosperous were naturally delighted with their new security; they believed that their wealth had saved them from the destitution and misery of badawah. But those who had fallen behind in the stampede for financial success felt lost and disoriented. The principles of muruwah seemed incompatible with market forces, and many felt thrust into a spiritual limbo. The old ideals had not been replaced by anything of equal value, and the ingrained communal ethos told them that this rampant individualism would damage the tribe, which could only survive if its members pooled all their resources.

Muhammad was born into the clan of Hashim, one of the most distinguished family groups in Mecca. His great-grandfather had been the first merchant to engage in independent trade with Syria and Yemen and the clan had the privilege of providing the pilgrims with water during the hajj, one of the most important offices in the city. But recently, Hashim had fallen on hard times. Muhammad's father

---

*The terms "clan" and "tribe" are not easy to distinguish from one another, but here "clan" refers to a family group *within* the tribe.

'Abdullah died before Muhammad was born and his mother Aminah was in such straitened circumstances that, it was said, the only Bedouin woman who was willing to be his wet nurse came from one of the poorest tribes in Arabia. He lived with her family until he was six years old, and would have experienced nomadic life at its harshest. Shortly after he was brought back to Mecca, his mother died. This double bereavement made a deep impression on Muhammad; as we shall see, he would always be concerned about the plight of orphans.

He was kindly treated by his surviving relatives. First he lived with his grandfather, 'Abd al-Muttalib, who had been a highly successful merchant in his prime. The old man made quite a favorite of Muhammad. He liked to have his bed carried outside, where he could lie in the shade of the Kabah, surrounded by his sons. Muhammad used to sit beside him, while his grandfather affectionately stroked his back. When he died, however, Muhammad, now eight years old, inherited nothing. His more powerful relatives controlled the estate and Muhammad went to live with his uncle Abu Talib, who was now the *sayyid* ("chief") of Hashim and greatly respected in Mecca, even though his business was failing. Abu Talib was very fond of his nephew, and his brothers also helped with Muhammad's education. Hamzah, the youngest, a man of prodigious strength, instructed Muhammad in the martial arts, making him a skilled archer and competent swordsman. His uncle 'Abbas, a banker, was able to get Muhammad a job managing the caravans on the northern leg of the journey to Syria.

The young Muhammad was well-liked in Mecca. He was handsome, with a compact, solid body of average height. His hair and beard were thick and curly, and he had a strikingly luminous expression and a smile of enormous charm, which is mentioned in all the sources. He was decisive and wholehearted in everything he did, so intent on the task at hand that he never looked over his shoulder, even if his cloak got caught in a thorny bush. When he did turn to speak to somebody, he used to swing his entire body around and address him full face. When he shook hands, he was never the first to withdraw his own. He inspired such confidence that he was known as al-Amin, the Reliable One. But his orphaned status constantly held him back. He had wanted to marry his cousin Fakhitah, but Abu Talib had to refuse his request for her hand, gently pointing out that Muhammad could not afford to support a wife, and made a more advantageous match for her.

But when Muhammad was about twenty-five years old, his luck suddenly changed. Khadijah bint al-Khuwaylid, a distant relative, asked him to take a caravan into Syria for her. She came from the clan of Asad, which was now far more influential than Hashim, and since her husband had died, she had become a successful merchant. Urban life often gives elite women the opportunity to flourish in business, though women of the lower classes had no status at all in Mecca. Muhammad conducted the expedition so competently that Khadijah was impressed and proposed marriage to him. She needed a new husband and her talented kinsman was a suitable choice: "I like you because of our relationship," she told him, "and your high reputation among your people, your trustworthiness, good character, and truthfulness."[18] Some of Muhammad's critics have sneered at this timely match with the wealthy widow, but this was no marriage of convenience. Muhammad loved Khadijah dearly, and even though polygamy was the norm in Arabia, he never took another, younger wife while she was alive. Khadijah was a remarkable woman, "determined, noble, and intelligent," says Ibn Ishaq, Muhammad's first biographer.[19] She was the first to recognize her husband's genius, and—perhaps because he had lost his mother at such a young age—he depended upon her emotionally and relied on her advice and support. After her death, he used to infuriate some of his later wives by endlessly singing her praises.

Khadijah was probably in her late thirties when she married Muhammad, and bore him at least six children. Their two sons—Al-Qasim and 'Abdullah—died in infancy, but Muhammad adored his daughters Zaynab, Ruqayyah, Umm Kulthum and Fatimah. It was a happy household, even though Muhammad insisted on giving a high proportion of their income to the poor. He also brought two needy boys into the family. On their wedding day, Khadijah had presented him with a young slave called Zayd ibn al-Harith from one of the northern tribes. He became so attached to his new master that when his family came to Mecca with the money to ransom him, Zayd begged to be allowed to remain with Muhammad, who adopted him and gave him his freedom. A few years later, Abu Talib was in such financial trouble that Muhammad took his five-year-old son 'Ali into his household to ease his burden.

He was devoted to both boys and treated them as his own sons.

We know very little about these early years. But from his later career it is clear that he had accurately diagnosed the malaise that was particularly rife among the younger generation, who felt ill at ease in this aggressive market economy. The Quraysh had introduced class distinctions that were quite alien to the muruwah ideal. Almost as soon as they had seized control of Mecca, the wealthier Quraysh had lived beside the Kabah, while the less prosperous inhabited the suburbs and the mountainous region outside the city. They had abandoned the badawah virtue of generosity and become niggardly, except that they called this shrewd business sense. Some no longer succumbed to the old fatalism, because they knew that they had succeeded in turning their fortunes around. They even believed that their wealth could give them some kind of immortality.[20] Others took refuge in a life of hedonism, making a religion out of pleasure.[21] Increasingly, it seemed to Muhammad that the Quraysh had jettisoned the best and retained only the worst aspects of muruwah: the recklessness, arrogance, and egotism that were morally destructive and could bring the city to ruin. He was convinced that social reform must be based on a new spiritual solution, or it would remain superficial. He probably realized, at some deep level, that he had exceptional talent, but what could he do? Nobody would take him seriously, because, despite his marriage to Khadijah, he had no real status in the city.

*

There was widespread spiritual restlessness. The settled Arabs, who lived in the towns and agricultural communities of the Hijaz, had developed a different kind of religious vision. They were more interested in gods than the Bedouin, but their rudimentary theism had no strong roots in Arabia. Very few mythical stories were told about the various deities. Allah was the most important god, and was revered as the lord of the Kabah, but he was a remote figure and had very little influence on the people's daily lives. Like the other "high gods" or "sky gods" who were a common feature of ancient religion, he had no developed cult and was never depicted in effigy.[22] Everybody knew that Allah had created the world; that he quickened each human embryo in the womb; and that he was the giver of rain. But these remained abstract beliefs. Arabs would sometimes pray to Allah in an emergency, but once the danger had passed they forgot all about him.[23] Indeed, Allah seemed like an irresponsible, absentee father; after he had brought men and women into being, he took no interest in them and abandoned them to their fate.[24]

The Quraysh also worshipped other gods. There was Hubal, a deity represented by a large, reddish stone which stood inside the Kabah.[25] There were three goddesses—Al-Lat, Al-Uzza and Manat—who were often called the "daughters of Allah" (*banat Allah*) and were very popular in the settled communities. Represented by large standing stones, their shrines in Ta'if, Nakhlah, and Qudhayd were roughly similar to the Meccan Haram. Although they were of lesser rank than Allah, they were often called his "companions" or "partners" and compared to the beautiful cranes (*gha-*

raniq) which flew higher than any other bird. Even though they had no shrine in Mecca, the Quraysh loved these goddesses and begged them to mediate on their behalf with the inaccessible Allah. As they jogged around the Kabah, they would often chant this invocation: "Al-Lat, Al-Uzza, and Manat, the third, the other. Indeed these are the exalted gharaniq; let us hope for their intercession."[26]

This idol worship was a relatively new religious enthusiasm, which had been imported from Syria by one of the Meccan elders who believed that they could bring rain, but we have no idea why, for example, the goddesses were said to be Allah's daughters—especially since Arabs regarded the birth of a daughter as a misfortune and often killed female infants at birth. The gods of Arabia gave their worshippers no moral guidance; even though they found the rituals spiritually satisfying, some of the Quraysh were beginning to find these stone effigies inadequate symbols of divinity.[27]

But what was the alternative? Arabs knew about the monotheistic religions of Judaism and Christianity. Jews had probably lived in Arabia for over a millennium, migrating there after the Babylonian and Roman invasions of Palestine. Jews had been the first to settle in the agricultural colonies of Yathrib and Khaybar in the north; there were Jewish merchants in the towns and Jewish nomads in the steppes. They had retained their religion, formed their own tribes but had intermarried with the local people, and were now practically indistinguishable from Arabs. They spoke Arabic, had Arab names, and organized their society in the same way as their Arab neighbors. Some of the Arabs had become Christians: there were important Christian communities in Yemen and along the frontier with Byzantium. The Meccan merchants had met Christian monks and hermits during their travels, and were familiar with the stories of Jesus and the concepts of Paradise and the Last Judgment. They called Jews and Christians the *ahl al-kitab* ("the People of the Book"). They admired the notion of a revealed text and wished they had sacred scripture in their own language.

But at this time, Arabs did not see Judaism and Christianity as exclusive traditions that were fundamentally different from their own. Indeed, the term "Jew" or "Christian" usually referred to tribal affiliation rather than to religious orientation.[28] These faiths were an accepted part of the spiritual landscape of the peninsula and considered quite compatible with Arab spirituality. Because no imperial power was seeking to impose any form of religious orthodoxy, Arabs felt free to adapt what they understood about these traditions to their own needs. Allah, they believed, was the God worshipped by Jews and Christians, so Christian Arabs made the hajj to the Kabah, the house of Allah, alongside the pagans. It was said that Adam had built the Kabah after his expulsion from Eden and that Noah had rebuilt it after the devastation of the Flood. The Quraysh knew that in the Bible the Arabs were said to be the sons of Ishmael, Abraham's oldest son, and that God had commanded Abraham to abandon him with his mother Hagar in the wilderness, promising that he would make their descendants a great people.[29] Later Abraham had visited Hagar and Ishmael in the desert and had rediscovered the shrine. He and Ishmael had rebuilt it yet again and designed the rites of the hajj.

Everybody knew that Arabs and Jews were kin. As the Jewish historian Josephus (37–c.100 CE) explained, Arabs circumcised their sons at the age of thirteen "because Ishmael, the founder of their nation, who was born to Abraham of the concubine [Hagar], was circumcised at that age."[30] Arabs did not feel it necessary to convert to Judaism or Christianity, because they believed that they were already members of the Abrahamic family; in fact, the idea of conversion from one faith to another was alien to the Quraysh, whose vision of religion was essentially pluralistic.[31] Each tribe came to Mecca to worship its own god, which stood in the Haram alongside the house of Allah. Arabs did not understand the idea of a closed system of beliefs, nor would they have seen monotheism as incompatible with polytheism. They regarded Allah, who was surrounded by the ring of idols in the Kabah, as lord of a host of deities, in much the same way as some of the biblical writers saw Yahweh as "surpassing all other gods."[32]

But some of the settled Arabs were becoming dissatisfied with this pagan pluralism, and were attempting to create an indigenous, Arabian monotheism.[33] Shortly before Muhammad received his first revelation, they had seceded from the religious life of the Haram. It was pointless, they told their tribesmen, to run round and round the Black Stone, which could "neither see, nor hear, nor hurt, nor help." Arabs, they believed, had "corrupted the religion of their father Abraham," so they were going to seek the *hanifiyyah*, his "pure religion."[34] This was not an organized sect. These hanifs all despised the worship of the stone effigies and believed that Allah was the only God, but not all interpreted this conviction identically. Some expected that an Arab prophet would come with a divine mission to revive the pristine religion of Abraham; others thought that this was unnecessary: people could return to the hanifiyyah on their own initiative; some preached the resurrection of the dead and the Last Judgment; others converted to Christianity or Judaism as an interim measure, until the *din Ibrahim* (the religion of Abraham) was properly established.

The hanifs had little impact on their contemporaries, because they were chiefly concerned with their own personal salvation. They had no desire to reform the social or moral life of Arabia, and their theology was essentially negative. Instead of creating something new, they simply withdrew from the mainstream. Indeed the word *hanif* may derive from the root *HNF*: "to turn away from." They had a clearer idea of what they did *not* want than a positive conception of where they were going. But the movement was a symptom of the spiritual restiveness in Arabia at the beginning of the seventh century, and we know that Muhammad had close links with three of the leading hanifs of Mecca. 'Ubaydallah ibn Jahsh was his cousin and Waraqah ibn Nawfal was a cousin of Khadijah: both these men became Christians. The nephew of Zayd ibn 'Amr, who attacked the pagan religion of Mecca so vehemently that he was driven out of the city, became one of Muhammad's most trusted disciples. It seems, therefore, that Muhammad moved in *hanafi* circles, and may have shared Zayd's yearning for divine guidance. One day, before he had been expelled from Mecca, Zayd had stood beside the Kabah inveighing against the corrupt religion of the Haram. But suddenly, he broke off. "Oh Allah!" he cried, "If I knew how you wished to be worshipped, I would so worship you, but I do not know."[35]

Muhammad was also seeking a new solution. For some years, accompanied by Khadijah, he had made an annual retreat on Mount Hira' during the month of Ramadan, distributing alms to the poor who visited him in his mountain cave and performing devotions.[36] We know very little about these practices, which were believed by some of the sources to have been inaugurated by Muhammad's grandfather. They seem to have combined social concern with rituals that may have included deep prostrations before Allah,[37] and intensive circumambulation of the Kabah. At this time, Muhammad had also started to have numinous dreams, radiant with hope and promise, that burst upon him "like the dawn of the morning," a phrase that in Arabic expresses the sudden transformation of the world when the sun breaks through the darkness in these eastern lands where there is no twilight.[38]

It was while he was making his annual retreat on Mount Hira' in about the year 610 that he experienced the astonishing and dramatic attack. The words that were squeezed, as if from the depths of his being, went to the root of the problem in Mecca.

> Recite in the name of your lord who created—
> From an embryo created the human.
>
> Recite your lord is all-giving

Who taught by the pen
Taught the human what he did not know before

The human being is a tyrant
He thinks his possessions make him secure
To your lord is the return of everything

This verse was an extension of the Quraysh's belief that Allah had created each one of them. It identified the proud self-sufficiency of muruwah as a delusion, because humans are entirely dependent upon God. Finally, Allah insisted that he was not a distant, absent deity but wanted to instruct and guide his creatures, so they must "come near" to him. But instead of approaching God in a spirit of prideful istighna', they must bow before him like a lowly slave: "Touch your head to the earth!" God commanded[39]—a posture that would be repugnant to the haughty Quraysh. From the very beginning, Muhammad's religion was diametrically opposed to some of the essential principles of muruwah.

When Muhammad came to himself, he was so horrified to think, after all his spiritual striving, that he had simply been visited by a jinni that he no longer wanted to live. In despair, he fled from the cave and started to climb to the summit of the mountain to fling himself to his death. But there he had another vision. He saw a mighty being that filled the horizon and stood "gazing at him, moving neither forward nor backward."[40] He tried to turn away, but, he said afterwards, "Towards whatever region of the sky I looked, I saw him as before."[41] It was the spirit (*ruh*) of revelation, which Muhammad would later call Gabriel. But this was no pretty, naturalistic angel, but a transcendent presence that defied ordinary human and spatial categories.

Terrified and still unable to comprehend what had happened, Muhammad stumbled down the mountainside to Khadijah. By the time he reached her, he was crawling on his hands and knees, shaking convulsively. "Cover me!" he cried, as he flung himself into her lap. Khadijah wrapped him in a cloak and held him in her arms until his fear abated. She had no doubts at all about the revelation. This was no jinni, she insisted. God would never play such a cruel trick on a man who had honestly tried to serve him. "You are kind and considerate to your kin," she reminded him. "You help the poor and forlorn and bear their burdens. You are striving to restore the high moral qualities that your people have lost. You honor the guest and go to the assistance of those in distress. This cannot be, my dear."[42] Muhammad and Khadijah had probably discussed their dawning understanding of the true nature of a religion that went beyond ritual performance and required practical compassion and sustained moral effort.

To reassure Muhammad, Khadijah consulted her cousin Waraqah, the hanif, who had studied the scriptures of the People of the Book and could give them expert advice. Waraqah was jubilant: "Holy! Holy!" he cried, when he heard what had happened. "If you have spoken the truth to me, O Khadijah, there has come to him the great divinity who came to Moses aforetime, and lo, he is the prophet of his people."[43] The next time Waraqah met Muhammad in the Haram, he kissed him on the forehead and warned him that his task would not be easy. Waraqah was an old man and not likely to live much longer, but he wished he could be alive to help Muhammad when the Quraysh expelled him from the city. Muhammad was dismayed. He could not conceive of a life outside Mecca. Would they really cast him out? he asked in dismay. Waraqah sadly told him that a prophet was always without honor in his own country.

It was a difficult beginning, fraught with fear, anxiety, and the threat of persecution. Yet the Qur'an has preserved another account of the experience on Mount Hira', in which the descent of the spirit is described as an event of wonder, gentleness, and peace, similar to the conception of Jesus in the womb of Mary.[44]

> We sent him down on the night of destiny
> And what can tell you of the night of destiny?
> The night of destiny is better than a thousand months
> The angels come down—the spirit upon her—
>   by permission of their lord from every order
> Peace she is until the rise of dawn.[45]

In this *surah* (chapter) of the Qur'an, there is a suggestive blurring of masculine and feminine, especially in pronouns, which is often lost in translation. In the Qur'an, the question "What can tell you?" regularly introduces an idea that would have been strange to Muhammad's first audience, indicating that they were about to enter the realm of the ineffable. Here Muhammad has self-effacingly disappeared from the drama of Mount Hira', and the night *(layla)* is center stage, like a woman waiting for her lover. The Night of Destiny had inaugurated a new era of communion between heaven and earth. The original terror of the divine encounter has been replaced by the peace that filled the darkness as the world waited for daybreak.

Muhammad would have understood the German historian Rudolf Otto, who described the sacred as a mystery that was both *tremendum* and *fascinans*. It was overpowering, urgent, and terrible, but it also filled human beings with "delight, joy, and a sense of swelling harmony and intimate intercourse."[46] Revelation cannot be described in a simple manner, and the complexity of his experience made Muhammad very cautious of telling anybody about it. After the experience on Mount Hira', there were more visions—we do not know exactly how many—and then, to Muhammad's dismay, the divine voice fell silent and there were no further revelations.

It was a time of great desolation. Had Muhammad been deluded after all? Was the presence simply a mischievous jinni? Or had God found him wanting and abandoned him? For two long years, the heavens remained obdurately closed and then, suddenly, the darkness was dispersed in a burst of luminous assurance:

> By the morning hours
> By the night when it is still

Your lord has not abandoned you
and does not hate you

What is after will be better
than what came before
To you the lord will be giving
You will be content

Did he not find you orphaned
    and give you shelter
Find you lost
    and guide you
Find you in hunger
    and provide for you

As for the orphan—
    do not oppress him
And one who asks for help—
    do not turn him away
And the grace of your lord—
    proclaim[47]

Here, Allah offered his assurance that he did not abandon his creatures, and reminded men and women to imitate his continuous kindness and generosity. Human beings, who had experienced the care of God, had a duty to help the orphan and the deprived.

Anybody who had known dereliction, hunger, and oppression must refuse under any circumstances to inflict this pain on others. The revelation concluded by telling Muhammad that it was time to "proclaim" this message to the Quraysh. But how would they respond?

Chapter Two

Jahiliyyah

He began quietly, speaking about his revelations to a small band of friends and family members, who became enthusiastic and sympathetic disciples, convinced that he was the long-awaited Arab prophet. But Muhammad realized that most of the Quraysh would find it well-nigh impossible to accept this. The messengers of Allah had all been towering figures, founding fathers of society. Some had even worked miracles. How could Muhammad measure up to Moses or Jesus? The Quraysh had watched him growing up; they saw him going about his business in the market, eating and drinking like everybody else. They had jettisoned many muruwah values, but had retained its elitist, aristocratic outlook and would expect God to choose a well-born karim from one of the more distinguished clans, rather than a minor member of Hashim. How would they react when Muhammad told them to abandon their lofty independence in a way that violated the sunnah of their forefathers?

Even at this early stage, Muhammad had encountered opposition. Khadijah, their daughters, 'Ali, and Zayd accepted his new status unconditionally, but though his uncle Abu Talib would continue to love and support him, he was deeply pained that Muhammad had the temerity to depart from the absolute authority of their ancestors. He was splitting up the family. Muhammad's cousins—Ja'far ibn Abi Talib, 'Abdullah and 'Ubaydallah ibn Jahsh, and their sister Zaynab—all accepted the revelations, but his uncles 'Abbas and Hamzah did not, though their wives did. Muhammad's son-in-law, Abu l-'As, who had married his daughter Zaynab, refused even to consider the new religion. Naturally, this was distressing to Muhammad. Family solidarity was a sacred value, and like any Arab, he respected the elders of his tribe and clan. He expected leadership to come from the top, but it was the younger generation who responded to his message. The revelations had already started to push Muhammad away from the norm. He could not help noticing that many of his followers came from the lower classes. A significant number were women, others freedmen, servants, and slaves. Foremost among the latter was Bilal, an Abyssinian with an extraordinarily loud voice. When the Muslims gathered to pray together in the Haram, Muhammad found himself surrounded by "the young men and weak people of the city."[1] Muhammad welcomed them warmly into his little company, but he must have wondered how a movement of such peripheral people could succeed. Indeed, some of the Qurayshan elders, who as yet knew nothing of the revelations, had begun to ask him why he was consorting with such riff-raff.

The "weak" people were not all down-and-outs; this technical tribal term denoted inferior tribal status rather than poverty. Muhammad's most zealous follower at this point was his friend 'Attiq Ibn 'Uthman, who was usually known by his *kunya*, Abu Bakr.* He was a successful, wealthy merchant, but like Muhammad he came from a "weak" clan that had fallen on hard times. Abu Bakr was "well-liked and of easy manners," Ibn Ishaq tells us, a kindly, approachable man, especially skilled in the interpretation of dreams.[2] Many of the younger generation, who were disturbed by the aggressive capitalism of Mecca, came to him for advice. Some of the young felt an urgent sense of personal peril, a torpor of depression from which they longed to wake, and a frightening alienation from their parents. The son of an important financier in one of the more powerful clans dreamed that his father was trying to push him into a pit that was filled with fire; then he had felt two strong hands pulling him to safety and realized, at the moment of waking, that his savior was Muhammad.[3] Another youth, this one from the prestigious clan of 'Abd Shams, came to Abu Bakr after dreaming that he had heard a voice crying aloud in the desert "Sleepers, awake!" and proclaiming that a prophet had appeared in Mecca.[4] Both these young men became Muslims, but the first kept his new faith a secret from his father for as long as he could, and the latter's conversion

---

*After the birth of their first son, Arabs customarily take an honorary title known as the *kunya*. Abu Bakr means "the father of Bakr." His wife would have been known as Umm Bakr, "the mother of Bakr." Muhammad was often known as Abu al-Qasim.

greatly displeased the elders of his clan, who were among the most influential men in Mecca.

The revelations had brought to light a fault line in the city. Over the years, a worrying divide had opened between young and old, rich and poor, men and women. This was dangerous. The scripture that was being revealed to Muhammad, verse by verse, surah by surah, condemned this kind of inequality; one faction would inevitably suffer at the hands of another.[5] Any society that was divided against itself would be destroyed, because it was going against the very nature of things. This was a frightening period. The incessant wars between Persia and Byzantium seemed to herald the end of the old world order, and even within Arabia, tribal warfare had reached chronic proportions. During the last twenty years, the ghazu, which had traditionally been short and sharp, had escalated into long, drawn out military campaigns as a result of unprecedented drought and famine. There was an apocalyptic sense of impending catastrophe. Muhammad was convinced that unless the Quraysh reformed their attitudes and behavior, they too would fall prey to the anarchy that threatened to engulf the world.

Under the inspiration of Allah, Muhammad was feeling his way towards an entirely new solution, convinced that he was not speaking in his own name, but was simply repeating the revealed words of God. It was a painful, difficult process. He once said: "Never once did I receive a revelation without thinking that my soul had been torn away from me."[6] Sometimes the message was clear. He could almost see and hear Gabriel distinctly. The words seemed to "come down" to him, like a shower of life-giving rain. But often the divine voice was muffled and obscure: "Sometimes it comes unto me like the reverberations of a bell, and that is the hardest upon me; the reverberations abate when I am aware of their message."[7] He had to listen to the undercurrent of events, trying to discover what was really going on. He would grow pale with the effort and cover himself with his cloak, as if to shield himself from the divine impact. He would perspire heavily, even on a cold day, as he turned inwards, searching his soul for a solution to a problem, in rather the same way as a poet has to open himself to the words that he must haul from the depths of himself to the conscious level of his mind. In the Qur'an, God instructed Muhammad to listen intently to each revelation as it emerged; he must be careful not to impose a meaning on a verse prematurely, before its full significance had become entirely clear.[8]

In the Qur'an, therefore, God spoke directly to the people of Mecca, using Muhammad as his mouthpiece, just as he spoke through the Hebrew prophets in the Jewish scriptures. Hence the language of the Qur'an is sacred, because—Muslims believe—it records the words spoken in some way by God himself. When Muhammad's converts listened to the divine voice, chanted first by the Prophet and later by the skilled Qur'an reciters, they felt that they had an immediate encounter with Allah. Biblical Hebrew is experienced as a holy tongue in rather the same way. Christians do not have this concept of a sacred language, because there is nothing holy about New Testament Greek; their scriptures presented Jesus as the

Word spoken by God to humanity. Like any scripture, the Qur'an thus provided an encounter with transcendence, bridging the immense gulf between our frail, mortal world and the divine.

Muhammad's converts eagerly awaited each new revelation; after he had recited it, they would learn it by heart, and those who were literate wrote it down. They felt moved and stirred by the exquisite language of their scripture, which, they were convinced, could only have come from God. It is difficult for a non-Arabic speaker to appreciate the beauty of the Qur'an, because this is rarely conveyed in translation. The text seems wearyingly repetitive; it has no apparent structure, no sustained argument or organizing narrative. But the Qur'an was not designed to be read sequentially. In its final form, the chapters or surahs of the Qur'an have been arranged arbitrarily, beginning with the longest and ending with the shortest, so the order is not important. Each surah contains essential teachings and it is possible to dip into the text at any point and imbibe crucial lessons.

In common with the majority of Arabs at this time, Muhammad could neither read nor write. The word *qur'an* means "recitation." It was not designed for private perusal, but like most scriptures, it was meant to be read aloud, and the sound was an essential part of the sense. Poetry was important in Arabia. The poet was the spokesman, social historian, and cultural authority of his tribe, and over the years the Arabs had learned how to listen to a recitation and had developed a highly sophisticated critical ear.[9] Bards chanted their odes at the annual trade fairs to excited audiences from all over the peninsula. Every year there was an important poetry contest at the fair of 'Ukaz, just outside Mecca, and the winning poems were embroidered in gold on fine black cloth and hung on the walls of the Kabah. Muhammad's followers would, therefore, have been able to pick up verbal signals in the text that are lost in translation. They found that themes, words, phrases, and sound patterns recurred again and again—like the variations in a piece of music, which subtly amplify the original melody, and add layer upon layer of complexity. The Qur'an was deliberately repetitive; its ideas, images, and stories were bound together by these internal echoes, which reinforced its central teaching with instructive shifts of emphasis. They linked passages that initially seemed separate, and integrated the different strands of the text, as one verse delicately qualified and supplemented others. The Qur'an was not imparting factual information that could be conveyed instantaneously. Like Muhammad, listeners had to absorb its teachings slowly; their understanding would grow more profound and mature over time, and the rich, allusive language and rhythms of the Qur'an helped them to slow down their mental processes and enter a different mode of consciousness.

The American scholar Michael Sells describes what happens when the driver of a hot, crowded bus in Egypt plays a cassette of Qur'anic recitations: "A meditative calm begins to set in. People relax. The jockeying for space ends. The voices of those who are talking grow quieter and less strained. Others are silent, lost in thought. A sense of shared community overtakes the discomfort."[10] Breath control is crucial to most of the contemplative traditions. Yogins have found that it brings a feeling of expansiveness, comparable to the effect of music, especially when played by oneself.[11] Qur'anic reciters chant long phrases on a slow exhalation and, when they inhale, leave silent pauses for meditation. It is natural for the audience to adjust their breathing too and find that this has a calming, therapeutic effect, which enables them to grasp the more elusive teachings of the text.

God was not booming clear instructions from on high. The divine voice constantly changed the way it referred to itself—as "we," "he," "your lord," "Allah" or "I"—shifting its relationship to both the Prophet and his audience. Nor was God distinctively male. Each recitation began with the invocation: "In the name of Allah, the Compassionate (*al-Rahman*) and the Merciful (*al-Rahim*)." Allah was a masculine noun, but the divine names al-Rahman and al-Rahim are not only grammatically feminine but related etymologically to the word for womb. A partially personified female figure was central to nearly all the early revelations. We find veiled allusions to a woman conceiving a child or giving birth; the image of a woman who has lost her only child, and the poignant evocation of a baby girl, murdered by her disappointed parents.[12] This strong female presence was remarkable in the aggressive patriarchy of Mecca and may explain why women were among the first to respond to the message of the Qur'an.

In each of the early surahs, God spoke intimately to the individual, often preferring to pose many of his teachings in the form of a question—"Have you not heard?" "Do you consider?" "Have you not seen?" Each listener was thus invited to interrogate him or herself. Any response to these queries was usually grammatically ambiguous or indefinite, leaving the audience with an image on which to meditate but with no decisive answer.[13] This new religion was not about achieving metaphysical certainty: the Qur'an wanted people to develop a different kind of awareness.

The Christian notion of the Last Judgment was central to the early message of the Qur'an. Muhammad believed that Mecca was in crisis because the Quraysh no longer felt accountable for their actions. In the steppes, the karim may have been arrogant and egotistic, but he had felt responsible for all the members of his tribe. The Quraysh, however, were busily amassing private fortunes, without giving a thought to the plight of the "weak." They did not seem to realize that their deeds would have long-lasting consequence. To counter this heedlessness, the Qur'an taught that individuals would have to explain their behavior to God. There would be a "day of reckoning" (*yawm ad-din*): the Arabic term also implies a "moment of truth."[14] At the end of their lives, human beings would have to face up to uncomfortable realities they had tried to avoid. They would experience a terrifying ontological reversal, in which everything that had seemed solid, important, and permanent would prove to be ephemeral. In staccato, lapidary verses, the early surahs tore this veil of delusion away.

> When the sun is overturned
> When the stars fall away

When the mountains are moved
When the ten-month pregnant camels are abandoned
When the beasts of the wild are herded together
When the seas are boiled over . . .
Then a soul will know what it has prepared.[15]

Sun, moon, and stars would disappear. Even a pregnant camel, the desert Arab's most precious possession, had no lasting value. All that really mattered was a person's conduct:

At that time people will straggle forth
   to be shown what they have done
Whoever does a mote's weight good will see it
Whoever does a mote's weight wrong will see it.[16]

Deeds that seemed unimportant at the time would prove to have been momentous; a tiny act of selfishness and unkindness or, conversely, an unconsidered act of generosity would become the measure of a human life: "To free a slave, to feed the destitute on a day of hunger, a kinsman, orphan, or a stranger out of luck, in need."[17]

Anybody who had performed these "works of justice" (*salihat*) would be rewarded eternally in Paradise (*'illiyyin*) but those who had concentrated on the selfish acquisition of material possessions would be punished in the *jahim*—a strange word, usually translated "raging fire." But the Qur'an was not preaching a crudely apocalyptic vision of hell. The passages describing the jahim are sad rather than angry.

Later Muslim tradition would elaborate on the themes of Heaven, Hell, and Judgment, but the Qur'an remains reticent, its language characteristically elusive and mysterious. More crucially, it compels the listener to face up to the judgment in the immediate present. The day of reckoning was not merely a distant event; it was also a "moment of truth" here and now. The probing, intimate questioning and the use of the present tense obliged listeners to face up to the implications of their behavior on a daily basis. What would it be like to know that you had wasted your time on earth when it was too late to do anything about it? The Qur'an asks insistently: "Where are you going with your life?"[18] Human beings were not inherently evil, but they were forgetful, all too eager to push these uncomfortable ideas to the back of their minds. So they needed a constant reminder (*dhikr*).[19] "Remind them," God urged Muhammad, "All you can do is be a reminder."[20]

People must, therefore, become self-aware, conscious of what they are doing. They must cultivate the virtue of *taqwa'*, a word that is sometimes translated "fear" but is better rendered "mindfulness." They must be continually on their guard against selfishness, greed, and arrogance. Instead of frightening themselves with the fear of hell, they should meditate on the signs (*ayat*) of God's generosity in the natural world and imitate his benevolence:

> Look at the camel
>   and how it is created
> Look at the sky and how it is raised

Look at the mountains and how they are set
Look at the earth and how it is spread.[20]

The entire cosmos was a veil, which hid the presence of its Creator. The succession of day and night, sun and moon, the life-giving rains, and the marvellous construction of the human being were all signs of God's presence. By contemplating these signs in a sustained and disciplined manner, they would become aware of the inexpressible reality behind them and be filled with gratitude.

At present the Quraysh despised the weak; they believed that failure and poverty revealed an inherent lack of nobility, so they felt no obligation towards the poor, the orphan, or the widow. But if they understood their dependence upon Allah at every moment of their lives, they would appreciate their own frailty, and their arrogance would be tempered by awe and wonder. They would lay aside their haughty self-reliance and their proudly cultivated refusal to bow to any creature, human or divine. Muhammad wanted every man, woman, and child in Mecca to develop within themselves the humble thankfulness that should characterize the human condition.

Muhammad was not content simply to work for social reform; he believed that without an interior transformation, a purely political program would be superficial. To effect this, he taught his little group the ritual actions that would enable them to cultivate this new attitude. First, they would meet for prayer *(salat)*: their devout prostration would be a daily reminder of their true condition. Salat interrupted their ordinary business and helped them to remember that

Allah was their first priority. It was very difficult for men and women schooled in the muruwah ethos to grovel like slaves, and many of the Quraysh were offended by this abject posture. But the physical routine of salat symbolized the surrender (*islam*) of their entire being to Allah. It taught their bodies at a level deeper than the rational to lay aside the self-regarding impulse to prance and preen arrogantly. A *muslim* was a man or a woman who had made this act of submission and was proud to be God's slave.

Second, members of the Muslim community (*ummah*) were required to give a proportion of their income in alms to the poor. This "pure offering" (*zakat*) took the egotism out of the traditional Bedouin generosity; instead of exhibiting their reckless, excessive liberality, they made a regular, undramatic contribution to the weaker members of the tribe. The new karim was no longer a person who gave away his entire fortune in a single night, but one who tirelessly practiced the "works of justice." At this stage, the new faith was called *tazakka* ("purification").[21] By looking after the poor and needy, freeing slaves, performing small acts of kindness on a daily, hourly basis, the Muslims learned to cloak themselves in the virtue of compassion and would gradually acquire a responsible, caring spirit, which imitated the generosity of Allah himself. If they persevered, they would purge their hearts of pride and selfishness and achieve a spiritual refinement.

For three years, Muhammad kept a low profile, preaching only to carefully selected people, but somewhat to his dismay, in 615 Allah instructed him to deliver his message to the whole clan of Hashim.[22] "The task is beyond my strength," he told 'Ali, but he went ahead and invited forty elders to a frugal meal. The meagre fare was a message in itself; there was to be no more excessive hospitality.[23] Luxury was not simply a waste of money but ingratitude, a thankless squandering of Allah's precious bounty. When the elders arrived, they were nonplussed when 'Ali served them a simple leg of mutton and a cup of milk. When he told the story later, 'Ali made it sound like Jesus' miracle of the loaves and fishes: even though there was scarcely enough for one person, everybody ate his fill. After the meal, Muhammad rose to address the gathering, told them about his revelations, and started to expound the principles of his religion of islam, but Abu Lahab, Abu Talib's half-brother, rudely interrupted him: "He's put a spell on you!" he cried, and the meeting broke up in disorder. Muhammad had to invite them back the following day and this time he managed to finish his presentation: "O sons of 'Abd al-Muttalib, I know of no Arab who has come to his people with a nobler message than mine." He concluded, "God has ordered me to call you to Him. So which of you will cooperate with me in this venture, as my brother, my executor, and my successor?"

There was an awkward silence, and the elders looked at one another in embarrassment. They could all remember Muhammad as a little boy, living on the charity of his relatives. How dared he claim to be the prophet of Allah? Even Muhammad's cousin Ja'far and his adopted son Zayd were reluctant to speak, but finally 'Ali, a gawky thirteen year old, could bear it no longer: "O prophet of God," he cried, "I will be your helper in this matter!" Muhammad laid his hand tenderly on the boy's neck: "This is my brother, my executor, and my successor among you," he said. "Hearken to him and obey him." This was too much. The spell was broken and the elders burst out laughing. "He's ordered you to listen to your son and obey him!" they cried derisively to Abu Talib as they stormed out of the house.[24]

Undeterred by this humiliating failure, Muhammad continued to preach more widely in the city, but with very little success. Nobody criticized his social message. They knew that muruwah required them to share their wealth with the poorer members of the tribe; it was one thing to *be* selfish and greedy, but quite another to *defend* these attitudes. Most people objected to the day of reckoning. This, they argued, was simply an old wives' tale. How could bodies that had rotted away in the earth come to life again? Was Muhammad seriously suggesting that their venerable ancestors would rise from their graves to "stand before the lord of all beings"?[25] The Qur'an replied that nobody could *prove* that there was no life after death, and that if Allah could create a human being out of a tiny drop of semen, he could easily resurrect a dead body.[26] It also pointed out that the people who poured scorn on the idea of a final reckoning were precisely those who had no intention of changing their oppressive, selfish behavior.[27] When faced with the insistent questioning of the Qur'an about the ultimate value of their life, they took refuge in denial and levity. But despite their skepticism, most of the Quraysh were content to leave Muhammad alone. They were businessmen who had little taste for ideological debate, and they knew that a serious internal conflict would be bad for trade. In any case, this little band of slaves, angry young men, and failing merchants was no real threat and their movement would surely peter out.

Muhammad himself was anxious to avoid an open rift. He had no desire to damage Mecca, the "mother of cities." He knew that some of the Quraysh thought that he wanted to become king—an abhorrent idea to the Arabs, who were deeply suspicious of monarchy. But Muhammad had no political ambitions. As if to reassure his critics, God told him firmly that he must not aspire to public office. He was simply a *nadhir*, a messenger with a warning, and should approach the Quraysh humbly, avoid provocation, and be careful not to attack their gods. This is what the great prophets had done in the past.[28] A prophet had to be altruistic; he must not trumpet his own opinions egotistically or trample on the sensibilities of others, but should always put the welfare of the community first. A prophet was first and foremost a *muslim*, one of "those who have surrendered themselves unto [Allah]."[29] In his desire to avoid a serious dispute, Muhammad did not, at this stage, emphasize the monotheistic content of his message. Like the hanifs, he was convinced that Allah was the only God, but he did not at first condemn the worship of the stone idols round the Kabah or the cult of the three gharaniq. Like most of the great religious sages, he was not much interested in orthodoxy.[30] Metaphysical speculation tended to make people quarrelsome and could be divisive. It was more important to practice the "works of justice" than to insist on a theological position that would offend many of the people he was trying to win over.

But tension was growing. In 616, some of the Quraysh attacked the Muslims while they were performing their ritual prayers in one of the glens outside the city. The incident shocked everybody in Mecca, and both sides desperately tried to reach a modus vivendi. This may have led to the notorious incident of the "satanic verses."[31] The episode is recounted by only two of Muhammad's early biographers, and some scholars believe it to be apocryphal, though it is hard to see why anybody would make it up. Both historians emphasize the desire for reconciliation in the city at this time. Ibn Sa'd starts his account by saying that in his desire to avoid an irrevocable breach with the Quraysh, Muhammad "sat down by himself, wishing that nothing be revealed to him that would drive them away."[32]

Tabari begins,

> When the apostle saw that his people had turned their backs
> on him and he was pained by their estrangement from what
> he had brought them from God, he longed that there should
> come to him from God a message that would reconcile his
> people to him. Because of his love for his people, and his anx-
> iety over them it would delight him that the obstacle that
> made his task so difficult could be removed; so he meditated
> on the project and longed for it, and it was dear to him.[33]

One day, Tabari continues, Muhammad was sitting beside the Kabah with some of the elders, reciting a new surah, in which Allah tried to reassure his critics: Muhammad had not intended to cause all this trouble, the divine voice insisted; he was not deluded nor inspired by a jinni; he had experienced a true vision of the divine and was simply telling his people what he had seen and heard.[34] But then, to his surprise, Muhammad found himself chanting some verses about the three "daughters of God": "Have you, then, ever considered what you are worshipping in Al-Lat and Al-Uzza, as well as Manat, the third, the other?" Immediately the Quraysh sat up and listened intently. They loved the goddesses who mediated with Allah on their behalf. "These are the exalted gharaniq," Muhammad continued, "whose intercession is approved."

Tabari claims that these words were put on his lips by the *shaytan* ("tempter"). This is a very alarming notion to Christians, who regard Satan as a figure of monstrous evil. The Qur'an is certainly familiar with the story of the fallen angel who defied God: it calls him Iblis (a contraction of the Greek *diabolos*: "devil"). But the shaytan who inspired this gracious compliment to the goddesses was a far less threatening creature. Shaytans were simply a species of jinn; they were "tempters" who suggested the empty, facile, and self-indulgent yearnings that deflected humans from the right path. Like all jinn, the shaytans were ubiquitous, mischievous, and dangerous, but not on a par with the devil. Muhammad had been longing for peace with the Quraysh; he knew how devoted they were to the goddesses and may have thought that if he could find a way of incorporating the gharaniq into his religion, they might look more kindly on his message. When he recited the rogue verses, it was his own desire talking—not Allah—and the endorsement of the goddesses proved to be a mistake. Like any other Arab, he naturally attributed his error to a shaytan.

Muhammad had not implied that the three "daughters of God" were on the same level as Allah. They were simply intermediaries, like the angels whose intercession is approved in the same surah.[35] Jews and Christians have always found such mediators compatible with their monotheism. The new verses seemed a truly propitious gesture and their effect on the Quraysh was electrifying. As soon as Muhammad had finished his recitation, he prostrated himself in prayer, and to his astonishment, the Qurayshan elders knelt down beside him, humbly pressing their foreheads to the ground. The news spread like wildfire through the city: "Muhammad has spoken of our gods in splendid fashion! He alleged in what he recited that they are the exalted gharaniq whose intercession is approved!"[36] The crisis was over. The elders told Muhammad: "We know that Allah kills and gives life, creates and preserves, but these our goddesses pray to Him for us, and since you have now permitted them to share divine honors with Him, we therefore desire to unite with you."[37]

But Muhammad was troubled. This was too easy. Were the Quraysh really going to amend their behavior, share their wealth with the poor, and be content to become the humble "slaves" of God? It did not seem likely. He was also disturbed by the jubilant words of the elders: he had certainly not meant to imply that the goddesses "shared divine honors" with Allah. While everybody else was celebrating, Muhammad went home, shut himself away, and meditated. That night Gabriel, the spirit of revelation, came to him: "What have you done, Muhammad?" he asked. "You have recited to those people something I did not bring you from God and have said what He did not say to you!"[38] Muhammad's wish for a compromise had distorted the divine message. He was immediately contrite, but God consoled him with a new revelation. All the previous prophets had made similar "satanic" mistakes. It was always a struggle to make sense of the revelations and all too easy to confuse the deeper current of inspiration with a more superficial idea of one's own. But, the revelation continued, "God renders null and void whatever aspersion the shaytan might cast, and God makes his messages clear in and by themselves."[39] An important principle had been established. God could alter his scriptures at the time that they were being revealed to a particular prophet. Revelation was progressive: We might say that Muhammad sometimes saw fresh implications in his message that qualified some of his earlier insights.

Now Muhammad had to go back to the Quraysh with a new verse that amended the "satanic" ones. Once again God asked: "Have you, then, ever considered what you are worshipping in Al-Lat and Al-Uzza, as well as in Manat?" But this time his answer was scathing. Why did they attribute daughters to Allah, when they themselves preferred sons? These so-called goddesses were simply "empty names," human projections fabricated by the Quraysh and their forefathers. Those who worship them follow "nothing but surmise and their own wishful thinking."[40] This was a slap in the face that not only eliminated the gharaniq but insulted the revered ancestors. Why did the Qur'an find it impossible to accommodate these three goddesses alongside the angels? Why ruin the chance of peace with this uncompromising rejection of an apparently harmless devotion?

After four years of Islam, Muslims could no longer take the traditional religion seriously. For most of the Quraysh, Allah was still a remote high god, who did not impinge on their daily lives. But this was no longer true for Muhammad's converts. The beauty of the Qur'an had made Allah a vibrant, indeed overwhelming reality. When they listened to their scripture, "a chill creeps over the skins of those who fear their Lord, and after a while, their skins and hearts soften at the remembrance of God."[41] The word of God was experienced as a powerful reality that could shatter the world: "Had We bestowed this Qur'an from on high upon a mountain," God told Muhammad, "thou wouldst see it humbling itself, breaking asunder for awe of God."[42] Allah was now completely different from the deity worshipped by the Quraysh and the "satanic verses" were wrong to suggest that Islam was the same as the old religion. It was ludicrous to imagine that the three stone idols of the gharaniq could influence the God of Islam.

The Qur'an now began to make this distinction clear. The other deities were as helpless and ineffective as dangerously weak tribal chiefs. They could not provide food for their worshippers, as Allah did, and they would not be able to intercede on behalf of their devotees on the day of reckoning.[43] Nothing was on a par with Allah.

*

Shortly after the repudiation of the "satanic verses," the Surah of Sincerity was revealed:

> Say he is God, one
> God forever
> Not begetting, unbegotten,
> and having as equal none.[44]

The principle of *tawhid* ("unity") became the crux of Muslim spirituality. It was not simply an abstract metaphysical affirmation of the singularity of the divine, but, like all Qur'anic teaching, a call to action. Because Allah was incomparable, Muslims must not only refuse to venerate the idols, but must also ensure that other realities did not distract them from their commitment to God alone: Wealth, country, family, material prosperity, and even such noble ideals as love or patriotism must take second place. Tawhid demanded that Muslims integrate their lives. In the struggle to make God their sole priority, a Muslim would glimpse, in the properly ordered self, the unity that was God. It was perhaps at this time that new converts were first required to utter the *shahadah*, the declaration of faith recited by all Muslims today: "I bear witness that there is no god but Allah and that Muhammad is his prophet."

The Quraysh would not have been shocked by monotheism per se, which was not, after all, a new idea to them. They had long found the religion of Jews and Christians compatible with their own traditions, and had not been particularly disturbed by the hanifs' attempt to create an authentically Arabian monotheism. But Muhammad was doing something different. Most hanifs had retained a deep respect for the Haram and had made no attempt to reform the social order. But in attacking the effigies that surrounded the Kabah, Muhammad implied that the Haram, on which the Meccan economy depended, was worthless. The Bedouin tribes did not make the hajj to visit the house of Allah but to pay their respects to their own tribal gods, whose cult was now condemned by the Qur'an in the strongest terms.[45] The Quraysh often invoked the "exalted gharaniq" as they circumambulated the Kabah; now this practice was dismissed as deluded and self-indulgent. Ta'if, where Al-Lat had her shrine, provided Mecca with its food; many of the Quraysh had summer homes in this fertile oasis. How could Ta'if remain on friendly terms with them if they condoned the insult to their goddess?

Overnight Muhammad had become the enemy. The Qurayshan leaders sent a delegation to Abu Talib, asking him to disown his nephew. Nobody could survive in Arabia without an official protector. A man who had been expelled from his clan could be killed with impunity, without fear of vendetta. Abu Talib, who was genuinely fond of Muhammad and not himself a Muslim, was in an impossible position. He tried to temporize, but the Quraysh returned with an ultimatum. "By God, we cannot endure that our fathers should be reviled, our customs mocked, and our gods insulted!" they cried. "Until you rid us of him, we will fight the pair of you until one side perishes." Abu Talib summoned Muhammad, begging him to stop this subversive preaching. "Spare me and yourself," he pleaded.

"Do not put upon me a burden greater than I can bear." Convinced that Abu Talib was about to abandon him, Muhammad replied with tears in his eyes: "O my uncle, by God if they put the sun in my right hand and the moon in my left on condition that I abandon this course, until God has made it victorious, or I perish therein, I would not abandon it." He then broke down and left the room, weeping bitterly. His uncle called him back. "Go and say what you please, for by God I will never give you up on any account."[46] For a while, Muhammad was safe. As long as Abu Talib remained his patron and could make this protection effective, nobody dared to touch him.

Abu Talib was a gifted poet and he now wrote passionate verses denouncing the clans who had deserted Hashim in its hour of need. The clan of al-Muttalib responded by declaring their solidarity with Hashim, but this good news was followed by a fateful defection. Abu Lahab, Abu Talib's half-brother, had opposed Muhammad and his revelations from the start, but to prevent a schism within the clan, he had betrothed two of his sons to Muhammad's daughters, Ruqayyah and Umm Kulthum. Now he forced his sons to repudiate the women. The elegant young Muslim aristocrat 'Uthman ibn 'Affan, however, had long admired Ruqayyah, one of the most beautiful girls in Mecca, and could now ask Muhammad for her hand.

The Qurayshan elders—especially those who had lost family members to Islam—now mounted a furious offensive against Muhammad. They would ostentatiously turn their backs whenever they heard Muslims praising Allah as the "one and only divine being," and aggressively demonstrate their joy when other deities were invoked.[47] They demanded that everybody remain faithful to the traditional faith. It was the only decent thing to do! All this talk of revelation was outrageous! Muhammad had made the whole thing up. Why should he alone, of all the Quraysh, have received a divine message?[48] Muhammad was mad; he had been led astray by a jinni; he was a sorcerer, who lured young people away from their fathers' sunnah by magic arts.[49] When he was asked to validate his claims by working a miracle—as Moses or Jesus had done—he admitted that he was an ordinary mortal like themselves.[50]

The leaders of the opposition included some of the most power-ful clan chiefs in Mecca. Foremost among them were Abu l-Hakam, an irascible, ambitious man, who seemed deeply disturbed by Islam; the elderly, corpulent Ummayah ibn Khalaf; and the highly intelli-gent Abu Sufyan, who had been a personal friend of Muhammad, together with his father in law 'Utbah ibn Rabi'ah and his brother. As yet Suhayl ibn 'Amr, chief of Amir—a devout man who, like Muhammad, made an annual retreat on Mount Hira'—had not yet made up his mind and Muhammad hoped to win him over. Some of the most able young men in Mecca were also virulently hostile to Islam: the warriors 'Amr ibn l-'As and Khalid ibn al-Walid, and—most zealous of all—'Umar ibn al-Khattab, the nephew of Abu l-Hakam, who was fanatically devoted to the old religion. While the other chiefs were proceeding cautiously against Muham-mad, 'Umar was ready for more extreme methods.

Muhammad had now given up hope of converting the Meccan establishment and realized that he must concentrate on the disaffected poorer people, who were eager for his message. This was an important turning point, which is recorded poignantly in the Qur'an. Muhammad had been so absorbed in a discussion with some of the Meccan grandees that he impatiently "frowned and turned away" when a blind man approached him with a question.[51] God reproved Muhammad severely: a prophet must approach *all* members of the community with the same respect. He must move beyond the aristocratic ethos of muruwah: the Qur'an was for rich and poor alike. In brushing the blind man aside as though he did not matter, Muhammad had behaved like a *kafir*.

The word *kafir* is often translated "unbeliever," but this is extremely misleading.[52] Muhammad had no quarrel with the beliefs of Abu l-Hakam and Abu Sufyan. In fact, much of their theology was quite correct. They believed without question, for example, that Allah was the creator of the world and the lord of the Kabah.[53] The trouble was that they did not translate their beliefs into action. They were impervious to the true meaning of the signs of God's benevolence in his creation, which required human beings to imitate him in all their dealings. Instead of despising and oppressing vulnerable people, they should behave like Allah and "spread over them the wings of tenderness."[54]

Kafir derives from the root *KFR* ("ingratitude"), which implies a discourteous refusal of something that is offered with great kindness and generosity. When God had revealed himself to the people of Mecca, some of them had, as it were, spat contemptuously in his face. The Qur'an does not berate the kafirun for their lack of religious conviction, but for their arrogance.[55] They are haughty and supercilious; they imagine that they are superior to the poorer, humbler people of Mecca, whom they consider second-class citizens and therefore worthy of contempt. Instead of realizing their utter dependence upon God, they still regard themselves as istighna'—self-reliant—and refuse to bow to Allah or anybody else. The kafirun are bursting with self-importance; they strut around haughtily, addressing others in an offensive, braying manner, and fly into a violent rage if they think that their honor has been impugned. They are so convinced that their way of life is better than anybody else's that they are particularly incensed by any criticism of their traditional lifestyle.[56] They sneer at Allah's revelation, perversely distorting the sense of the Qur'an simply to display their cleverness.[57] They were unable even to consider anything new: their hearts were "veiled," "rusted over," "sealed" and "locked."[58]

The chief vice of the kafirun was *jahiliyyah*. Muslims have traditionally used this term to refer to the pre-Islamic period in Arabia and so it is usually translated "the Time of Ignorance." But although the root *JHL* has some connotations of "ignorance," its primary meaning is "irascibility": an acute sensitivity to honor and prestige; arrogance, excess, and above all, a chronic tendency to violence and retaliation.[59] Jahili people were too proud to make the surrender of Islam; why *should* a karim moderate his behavior and act like a slave ('abd), praying with his nose on the ground and treating the base-born like equals? The Muslims called Abu l-Hakam, their chief enemy, "Abu Jahl" not because he was ignorant of Islam—he understood it all too well—but because he fought Islam arrogantly, with blind, fierce, and reckless passion. But the tribal ethos was so engrained that, as we shall see, Muslims continued to exhibit jahili symptoms long after they had converted to Islam. Jahiliyyah could not be eradicated overnight, and it remained a latent menace, ready to flare up destructively at any moment.

Instead of succumbing to the jahili spirit, the Qur'an urges Muslims to behave with *hilm*, a traditional Arab virtue. Men and women of hilm were forbearing, patient, and merciful.[60] They could control their anger and remain calm in the most difficult circumstances instead of exploding with rage; they were slow to retaliate; they did not hit back when they suffered injury, but left revenge to Allah.[61] Hilm also inspired positive action: if they practiced hilm, Muslims would look after the weak and disadvantaged, liberate their slaves, counsel each other to patience and compassion, and feed the destitute, even when they were hungry themselves.[62] Muslims must always behave with consummate gentleness and courtesy. They were men and women of peace: "For true servants of the Most Gracious are they who walk gently on the earth, and who, whenever the jahilun address them, reply 'Peace' (*salam!*)"[63]

After the affair of the "satanic verses," the conflict with the kafirun became very nasty. Abu Jahl regularly subjected any Muslims he met to vitriolic verbal abuse and slandered them with vicious lies and rumor; he threatened merchants with ruin, and simply beat up the "weaker" Muslims. The kafirun could not hurt Muslims who had strong protectors, but they could attack slaves and those who lacked adequate tribal patronage. Ummayah, chief of Jumah, used to torture Bilal, his Abyssinian slave, by tying him up and forcing him to lie exposed to the gruelling sun, with a huge boulder on his chest. Abu Bakr could not bear to watch Bilal suffering, so he bought him from Ummayah and set him free. He also liberated a Muslim slave girl, when he saw 'Umar ibn al-Khattab flogging her. Some of the younger Muslims were locked up by their families, who even tried to starve them into submission. The situation became so serious that Muhammad sent the more vulnerable members of the ummah to Abyssinia, where the Christian governor gave them asylum. It was becoming painfully clear that, unthinkable as it might seem, there might be no future for the Muslims in Mecca.

It must have been very difficult indeed for the Muslims, brought up in the jahili spirit, to practice hilm and turn the other cheek. Even Muhammad sometimes had to struggle to maintain his composure. One of the early surahs expresses his rage against his uncle Abu Lahab and his wife, who used to scatter sharp thorns outside his house.[64] On one occasion, Muhammad overheard some of the Qurayshan chiefs jeering at him contemptuously while he was circumambulating the Kabah. For a while he was able to keep his rising anger in check, but by the time he had completed the third circuit, his face was as black as thunder. He stopped in his tracks, faced the kafirun, and, instead of wishing them "Peace," as the Qur'an enjoined, said grimly: "Will you listen to me, O Quraysh. By him who holds my life in His hand, I bring you slaughter!" He uttered the last word so threateningly that the chiefs were silenced. But the next day, they had recovered their nerve. They leapt on Muhammad when he arrived in the Haram, encircled him menacingly, and started to rough him up, pulling him about by his robe. This time, Muhammad did not respond aggressively, but allowed the chiefs to manhandle him, until Abu Bakr intervened, weeping: "Would you kill a man for saying Allah is my lord?"[65]

But this kind of behavior could sometimes be counterproductive. One day, Abu Jahl came upon Muhammad near the Safa Gate, an important site of the hajj, and was so incensed to see him calmly occupying this sacred spot that he exploded in true jahili style. Again, Muhammad refused to retaliate, but sat and listened to the string of devastating insults without uttering a word. Finally Abu Jahl ended his tirade and went to join some of the other chiefs in the Haram, while Muhammad went sadly and silently home. But that evening, his uncle Hamzah, who had been out hunting, heard what had happened and became incandescent with fury. He set off immediately to find Abu Jahl, and hit him hard with his bow. "Will you insult him when I follow his religion?" he yelled. "Hit me back if you can!" Loath to take on Hamzah, whose physical strength was legendary in Mecca, Abu Jahl hastily restrained his companions, admitting that he had grievously insulted Muhammad.[66]

Hamzah became a devout Muslim, but this was not exactly the way that Muhammad would have wished his uncle to enter Islam. Toward the end of 616, there was another, even more surprising conversion. 'Umar ibn al-Khattab had decided that it was time to kill Muhammad, and strode through the streets of Mecca, sword in

hand, toward a house at the foot of Mount Safa, where he heard that
the Prophet was spending the afternoon. He did not know that his
sister Fatimah bint al-Khattab and her husband had secretly become
Muslims. Thinking that 'Umar was safely out of the way, they had
invited one of the few literate Muslims to come and recite the latest
surah. But on his way to Mount Safa, 'Umar was intercepted by another Muslim, who fearing for Muhammad's life, informed 'Umar
that his own sister had converted to Islam. 'Umar rushed home, and
was horrified to hear the words of the Qur'an issuing from an up-
stairs window. "What is this balderdash!" he roared as he burst into
the room. The reciter fled in terror, dropping the manuscript in his
haste, while 'Umar threw his sister to the ground. But when he saw
that she was bleeding, he felt ashamed, picked up the manuscript,
and began to read the surah. 'Umar was one of the judges of the
poetry competition in 'Ukaz, and realized at once that he was looking at something unique. This was quite different from a conventional Arabic ode. "How fine and noble is this speech," he exclaimed
with wonder, and immediately the beauty of the Qur'an diffused his
rage and touched a core of receptivity deeply buried within him. Yet
again he grabbed his sword, and ran through the streets to the house
where Muhammad was. "What has brought you, Ibn al-Khattab?"
asked the Prophet. "I have come to you to believe in God his
apostle and what he has brought from God." replied.
Muhammad gave thanks so loudly that every one out of hiding house, who
had dived for cover as soon as they s
scarcely able to believe what h

Ibn Ishaq has recorded another, less dramatic but equally significant version of 'Umar's conversion. He had set out to join some friends for a drink in the market one evening, but when his friends failed to turn up, decided to perform the tawaf instead. The Haram was entirely deserted, except for Muhammad, who was standing close to the Kabah, reciting the Qur'an quietly to himself. 'Umar decided that he wanted to listen, so he crept under the damask cloth that covered the shrine and edged his way round until he was standing directly in front of Muhammad. As he said later: "There was nothing between us but the cover of the Kabah"—all his defenses but one were down. Then the power of the Qur'an did its work: "When I heard the Qur'an, my heart was softened and I wept, and Islam entered into me."[68] 'Umar's conversion was a bitter blow to the opposition, but because he was protected by his clan, there was nothing that they could do to hurt him.

Abu Jahl now imposed a boycott on the clans of Hashim and al-Muttalib: nobody could marry into them or trade with them—they could not even sell them food. All the members of Hashim and al-Muttalib, Muslim and non-Muslim alike, moved into Abu Talib's street, which became a little ghetto. When Muhammad's household aᳵ ᳵ ᳵ Abu Lahab and his family moved out and took up residence in the ᳵ ᳵ ᳵt of 'Abd Shams. The purpose of the boycott was not to starve ᳵ ᳵ ᳵ clans, but to bring home to them the consequence of removing ᳵ ᳵ ᳵs from the tribe. If Muhammad wanted to withdraw from ᳵ ᳵ ᳵ life of Mecca, he could not continue to benefit from the economy.[69] The ban collapsed after three years. It was especially unpopular among those who had relatives in Hashim or al-Muttalib, and could not in good conscience allow them to go hungry. Muslims like Abu Bakr and 'Umar, who did not belong to the proscribed clans, sent provisions whenever they could. One Meccan regularly loaded a camel with supplies, led it to Abu Talib's street under cover of night, gave the beast a thwack on its hind-quarters, and sent it lumbering down the alley. On one occasion, Abu Jahl accosted one of Khadijah's nephews, who was making his way to the ghetto with a bag of flour. There was soon a fierce argument. Another Qurayshi joined in, disgusted that Abu Jahl was prevent-ing a man from taking food to his aunt, and gave him a huge blow with a camel's jaw that knocked him to the ground.

During this ban, the Qur'an reminded the Muslims that other prophets—Joseph, Noah, Jonah, Moses, and Jesus—had also warned their people to reform their behavior, and when they refused, their societies had collapsed, because they were not acting in accordance with the fundamental principles of the universe.[70] Unlike animals, fish, or plants, which are natural muslims since they submit instinct-ively to these basic laws, human beings have free will.[71] When they oppress the weak and refuse to share their wealth fairly with the poor, this violation of God's law is as unnatural as though a fish were to try to live on dry land. Disaster was inevitable. But the Qur'an continued to urge Muslims to be patient and not seize this oppor-tunity for a personal vendetta against their enemies.

Some of the Quraysh too were anxious for peace. Shortly after the imposition of the ban, a small delegation had approached Muhammad, led by a venerable elder who was too close to death to be personally threatened by the Prophet. He suggested a compromise: the whole city could worship Allah one year and the other gods the next. But Muhammad could not accept this offer. Instead, the Surah al-Kafirun proposed peaceful coexistence:

> You who reject the faith (kafirun)
> I do not worship what you worship
> And you do not worship what I worship
> I am not a worshipper of what you worship
> You are not a worshipper of what I worship.
> A reckoning (din) for you and a reckoning for me.[72]

People worship different things; there must be "no coercion in matters of faith!" (*la ikra fi'l-din!*)[73] Din meant "reckoning," but also "religion," "way of life," or "moral law." Each individual had his or her own din and there was no need for force or compulsion.

In the end, blood loyalty led to the end of the boycott. Four of the Qurayshan establishment, who had relatives in Hashim and al-Muttalib, solemnly requested an end to the ban, and despite the angry protests of Abu Jahl, the other chiefs agreed. There must have been great rejoicing in the Muslim community. When they heard the news, some of the emigrants came home from Abyssinia, convinced that the worst was over. But they had been too optimistic. Early in 619, Khadijah died. She was aging, and her health may have been irreparably damaged by the food shortages. She had been Muhammad's closest companion, and nobody—not even Abu Bakr or the fervent 'Umar—would ever be able to provide Muhammad with the same intimate support. The early biographers call 619 Muhammad's "year of sadness." Not long afterwards, a second death had even more far reaching implications. Abu Talib had been ruined financially, and may also have been physically weakened by the boycott. Later that year, he fell ill and died. And the new chief of Hashim was Abu Lahab.

Chapter Three

Hijrah

EVERYBODY IN MECCA was immediately aware of Muhammad's new vulnerability. Abu Lahab did not repudiate Muhammad: a chief was expected to give all his clansmen a measure of protection and to fail in this duty at the very start of his office would have been a sign of weakness. But it was obvious that he extended his patronage very grudgingly. Muhammad's neighbors played disgusting tricks with a sheep's uterus, thwacking him with it while he was at prayer, and once even dropping it into the family cooking pot. One day, a young Qurayshi threw filth all over Muhammad while he was walking in the city. When his daughter Fatimah saw him in this state, she burst into tears. "Don't cry, my little girl," Muhammad reassured her tenderly, while she tried to clean him up. "God will protect your father." But to himself, he added grimly: "Quraysh never treated me thus while Abu Talib was alive."[1]

His weakness probably affected the position of some of the more vulnerable Muslims. Abu Bakr, for example, had been almost ruined by the boycott. He lived in the district of the Jumah clan, and its chief, the corpulent Ummayah ibn Khalaf who used to expose Bilal to the sun, now felt free to do the same to Abu Bakr, tying him to his young cousin and leaving them, parched and sick, in this humiliating position in the sweltering heat. Taym, their clan, was too weak to protect them, so, realizing that he had no future in Mecca, Abu Bakr set off to join the Muslim emigrant community in Abyssinia. But on the road, he met Ibn Dughunnah, one of the Bedouin allies of the Quraysh, who was horrified to hear what had happened. He insisted on returning to Mecca, and formally took Abu Bakr under his own protection. Since the Qurayshan establishment was anxious to cultivate Ibn Dughunnah, they agreed to this arrangement, but asked him to make sure that Abu Bakr did not pray or recite the Qur'an in public. He was so popular and charismatic, they explained, that he would lure the young men away from the official religion. So Abu Bakr worshipped alone, making a little *masjid*, a place for prostration, in front of his house.

But the situation was clearly unsatisfactory. Muhammad tried to find a new protector for himself in the pleasant, fertile oasis of Ta'if, but it was a hopeless venture, which revealed the measure of his desperation, because the tribe of Thaqif had been greatly offended by Muhammad's repudiation of their goddess Al-Lat. Muhammad visited three of the leaders of Thaqif, asking them to accept his religion and extend their protection to him, but they were so enraged by his effrontery that they had their slaves chase him through the streets.

He was only able to escape by diving into the garden of 'Utbah ibn Rabi'ah, one of the chief Meccan kafirun, who had a summer home in Ta'if. 'Utbah and his brother Shaybah saw Muhammad's humiliating flight, but did not wish to hand a fellow-tribesman over to the Thaqif. So instead of reporting Muhammad, they sent a slave to him with a platter of grapes.

Crouching ignominiously behind a tree, Muhammad was close to despair. It was customary for Arabs to "take refuge" with a god or a jinni in times of crisis, so now Muhammad took refuge with Allah.

> Oh God, to Thee I complain of my weakness, my little re-source and lowliness before men. O Most Merciful, Thou art lord of the weak and Thou art my lord. To whom wilt Thou confide me? To one afar, who will misuse me? Or an enemy to whom Thou hast given power over me? If Thou art not angry with me, I care not. Thy favor is more wide for me. I take refuge in the light of Thy countenance by which the darkness is illumined, and the things of this world and the next are rightly ordered, lest Thy anger descend upon me or Thy wrath light upon me. It is for Thee to be satisfied until Thou art well-pleased. There is no power and no might save in Thee.[2]

It is unusual for Ibn Ishaq to give such an intimate account of Muhammad's state of mind. It indicates a moment of spiritual truth. In this act of islam, Muhammad realized more fully than ever before that he had no security and no true protector but Allah.

God seemed to answer his prayer, because no sooner had he finished speaking, than 'Addas, 'Utbah's slave boy, arrived with the grapes. He was a Christian, and Muhammad was delighted to learn that he came from Nineveh, the city of the prophet Jonah. He told 'Addas that Jonah was his brother, because he was a prophet, too. 'Addas was so overwhelmed that, to the disgust of 'Utbah, who was watching the encounter, he kissed Muhammad's head, hands, and feet. After this unexpected encounter with one of the People of the Book, Muhammad felt less isolated. It reminded him that, even though the Arabs had rejected him, there was a multitude of worshippers in the great world outside Arabia who would understand his mission. He felt cheered as he began his homeward journey, and stopped to pray in the small oasis of Nakhlah, where he was overheard by a group of "unseen beings" (jinn). The word jinn did not always refer to the whimsical sprites of Arabia; it could also be used for "strangers," people who had hitherto been unseen. The Qur'an indicates that the travellers, who lurked out of sight in Nakhlah, listening to Muhammad's recitation, may have been Jews. They were so overcome by the beauty and felicity of the Arabic scripture that when they returned home, they told their people that they had heard "a revelation bestowed from on high, after [that of] Moses," which confirmed the truth of the Torah and would guide human beings to the right path.[3]

Muhammad's horizons were beginning to expand. He had been certain that he had been sent simply as a "warner" (nadhir) to his own tribe and that Islam was only for the people of Mecca. But now he was beginning to look further afield to the People of the Book, who had received earlier revelations. Despite the confidence that this gave him, he was now desperate. Once the kafirun had learned of his attempt to find support in Ta'if, his position would be even more precarious, so before entering Mecca, he sent word to three clan chiefs, asking for their patronage. Two refused, but the third—Mu'tim, chief of Nawfal, who had been one of those who had campaigned to end the boycott—promised to protect Muhammad, and he was now able to return home.

But this could not be a long-term solution. Somehow Muhammad had to win over the Quraysh. In 619, he began to preach to the pilgrims and merchants who attended the trade fairs that culminated in the hajj. Perhaps, like Abu Bakr, he would find a Bedouin protector, and if the Qurayshan establishment saw that he was respected by their Bedouin confederates, they might learn to accommodate him. But the Bedouin pilgrims were hostile and insulting. The last thing they wanted was a religion that preached submission and humility. Muhammad must have felt that he had come to the end of his resources. He was still grieving for Khadijah; his position in Mecca was desperately precarious; and after preaching for seven years, he had made no real headway. Yet at this low point of his career, he had the greatest personal mystical experience of his life.

He had been visiting one of his cousins who lived near the Haram, so he decided to spend the night in prayer beside the Kabah, as he loved to do. Eventually he went to sleep for a while in the enclosed area to the northwest of the shrine, which housed the tombs of Ishmael and Hagar. Then, it seemed to him that he was awakened by Gabriel and conveyed miraculously to Jerusalem, the holy city of the Jews and Christians—an experience that may have been recorded by this oblique verse of the Qur'an:

> Limitless in His glory is He who transported His servant by night from the Inviolable House of Worship (*al masjid al-haram*) to the Remote House of Worship (*al-masjid al-aqsa*)—the environs of which We had blessed—so that We might show him some of Our symbols (ayat).[4]

Jerusalem is not mentioned by name, but later tradition associated the "Remote House" with the holy city of the People of the Book, the Jews and the Christians. According to the historian Tabari, Muhammad told his companions that he had once been taken by the angels Gabriel and Michael to meet his "fathers": Adam (in the first heaven) and Abraham (in the seventh), and that he also saw his "brothers": Jesus, Enoch, Aaron, Moses, and Joseph.[5] The Qur'an also claimed that Muhammad had a vision beside the "lote tree" which marked the limit of human knowledge:

> He saw it descending another time
> at the lote tree of the furthest limit
> There was the garden of sanctuary
> When something came down over the lote tree enfolding

His gaze did not turn aside nor go too far
He had seen the sight of his lord, great signs (ayat)[6]

The Qur'an is reticent about this vision. He saw only God's signs and symbols—not God himself, and later mystics emphasized the paradox of this transcendent insight, in which Muhammad both saw and did not see the divine essence.

Later Muslims began to piece together these fragmentary references to create a coherent narrative. Influenced perhaps by the stories told by Jewish mystics of their ascent through the seven heavens to the throne of God, they imagined their prophet making a similar spiritual flight. The first account of this "night journey" (*'isra*) is found in the eighth-century biography by Ibn Ishaq. In this extended story, Gabriel lifted the Prophet onto a heavenly steed and together they flew through the night to Jerusalem, where they alighted on the site of the ancient Jewish Temple, the "Remote House" of the Qur'an. There they were greeted by Abraham, Moses, Jesus, and all the great prophets of the past, who welcomed Muhammad into their fellowship and invited him to preach to them. Afterwards the prophets all prayed together. Then a ladder was brought and Muhammad and Gabriel climbed to the first of the seven heavens and began their ascent to the divine throne. At each stage, Muhammad met and conversed with some of the greatest of the prophets. Adam presided over the first heaven, where Muhammad was shown a vision of Hell; Jesus and John the Baptist were in the second heaven; Joseph in the third; Enoch in the fourth; Moses and

Aaron in the fifth and sixth, and finally Muhammad met Abraham in the seventh, on the threshold of the divine realm.

Most writers leave the final vision of God in reverent obscurity, because it was literally ineffable, lying beyond the reach of speech. Muhammad had to abandon ordinary human concepts, going beyond the lote tree, the boundary of mundane knowledge. Even Gabriel could not accompany him on this last stage of his journey. He had to leave everybody and—the later mystics insisted—even himself behind to lose himself in God. The story of the night journey and the heavenly ascent is an event that—in some sense—happened once, but which also happens all the time. It represented a perfect act of islam, a self-surrender that was also a return to the source of being. The story became the paradigm of Muslim spirituality, outlining the path that all human beings must take, away from their preconceptions, their prejudices, and the limitations of egotism.

The vision did not result in a Qur'anic revelation; it was a personal experience for the Prophet himself. But placed as it is by the early biographers at this particular moment of Muhammad's life, it is a wonderful commentary on the deeper subtext of these external events. Muhammad was being compelled by circumstances over which he had little control to leave Mecca and everything that was dear and familiar to him—at least for a while. He had to move beyond his original expectations, and transcend the received ideas of his time. In the traditional Arabian ode, the poet usually began with a dhikr, a "remembrance" of his lost beloved, who was travelling with her tribe further and further away from him. In the next section, the bard embarked on a "night journey," breaking out of his nostalgic reverie, and setting off alone across the steppes on his camel—a fearful trek during which he had to confront his own mortality. Finally, the poet was reunited with his tribe. In the final section of the ode, he proudly boasted of the heroic values of his people, their prowess in battle, and their ceaseless war against all strangers who threatened their survival.[7] In Muhammad's night journey, these old muruwah values were reversed. Instead of returning to his tribe, the prophet travelled far away from it to Jerusalem; instead of asserting his tribal identity with the arrogant chauvinism of jahiliyyah, Muhammad surrendered his ego. Instead of rejoicing in fighting and warfare, Muhammad's journey celebrated harmony, transcendence of the blood group, and integration with the rest of humanity.

The story of the night journey reveals Muhammad's longing to bring the Arabs of the Hijaz, who had felt that they had been left out of the divine plan, into the heart of the monotheistic family. This is a story of pluralism. Muhammad was abandoning the pagan pluralism of Mecca, because it had degenerated into the self-destructive arrogance and violence of jahiliyyah, but he was beginning to embrace monotheistic pluralism. In Jerusalem, he discovered that all the prophets, sent by God to all peoples, are "brothers." Muhammad's prophetic predecessors do not spurn him as a pretender, but welcome him into their family. The prophets do not revile or try to convert each other; instead they listen to each other's insights. They invite the new prophet to preach to them, and, in one version of the story,

Muhammad asks Moses for advice about how frequently Muslims should pray. Originally, God wanted salat fifty times a day, but Moses kept sending Muhammad back to God until the number of prescribed prayers had been reduced to five (which Moses still found excessive).[8] The fact that this appreciation of other traditions is written into the archetypal myth of Muslim spirituality shows how central this pluralism was to early Islam.

From this point, the Qur'an began to emphasize this shared vision. In one remarkable passage, Allah makes it clear that the faithful must believe indiscriminately in the revelations of every single one of God's messengers:

> Say: We believe in God, and in that which has been bestowed from on high upon us, and that which has been bestowed upon Abraham and Ishmael and Isaac and Jacob and their descendents, and that which has been vouchsafed by their Sustainer unto Moses and Jesus and all the [other] prophets: we make no distinction between any of them. And unto Him do we surrender ourselves (*lahu muslimun*).[9]

You could not be a muslim unless you also revered Moses and Jesus. True faith required surrender to God, not to an established faith. Indeed, exclusive loyalty to only one tradition could become *shirk*, an idolatry which puts a human institution on the same level as God. This is one of the first passages in the Qur'an to emphasize the words "islam" and "muslim," which both derive from the verb *aslama*: "surrendering oneself entirely to someone else's will."[10] The verse continues:

> For if one goes in search of a religion other than self-surren-
> der (islam) unto God, it will never be accepted from him, and
> in the life to come, he shall be among the lost.[11]

This verse is often quoted to "prove" that the Qur'an claims that Islam is the one, true faith and that only Muslims will be saved. But "Islam" was not yet the official name for Muhammad's religion, and when this verse is read correctly in its pluralistic context, it clearly means the exact opposite.

The Qur'an depicts one prophet handing on the revelation to another. The message passes from Abraham to Ishmael and Isaac to Moses, and so on, in a continuous narrative. The Qur'an is simply a "confirmation" of the previous scriptures,[12] and the Torah, the Gospel, and the Qur'an are simply moments in God's continuous self-disclosure: "Verily, those who have attained to faith [in this divine writ], as well as those who follow the Jewish faith, and the Sabians,* and the Christians—all who believe in God and the Last Day and do righteous deeds—no fear need they have, and neither shall they grieve."[13] There was no thought of forcing everybody into the Muslim ummah. Each of the revealed traditions had its own din, its

---

*The Sabians are thought to be a monotheistic sect in southern Arabia (modern Yemen), though some commentators believe that the Qur'an refers here to the Zoroastrians of the Persian empire.

own practices, and insights. "Unto every one of you have We appointed a [different] law and way of life," God told Muhammad:

> And if God had so willed, He could surely have made you all one single community: but [He willed it otherwise] in order to test you by means of what he has vouchsafed unto you. Vie, then, with one another in doing good works! Unto God you must all return; and then He will make you truly understand all that on which you were wont to differ.[14]

God was not the exclusive property of one tradition, but was the source of all human knowledge: "God is the light of the heavens and the earth," Allah explained in one of the most mystical verses in the Qur'an. The divine light could not be confined to any individual lamp, but was common to them all, enshrined in every one of them:

> The parable (ayah) of this light is, as it were, that of a niche containing a lamp; the lamp is [enclosed in glass], the glass [shining] like a radiant star: [a lamp] lit from a blessed tree—an olive tree that is neither of the east nor the west—the oil whereof [is so bright that it] would well-nigh give light [of itself], even though fire had not touched it—light upon light.[15]

The olive tree signifies the continuity of revelation, which springs from one root but branches into a multitudinous variety of religious

experience that cannot be confined to a single faith or locality, and
is neither of the east nor the west.

Muhammad's position in Mecca remained dangerously insecure.
During the hajj of 620, he again visited the pilgrims who were camp-
ing in the valley of Mina, going from tent to tent in the hope of at-
tracting support and protection. This time, instead of wholesale
rejection, he met a group of six Arabs from Yathrib, who had camped
in the gully of 'Aqabah. As usual, Muhammad sat with them, explained his mission and recited the Qur'an, but this time, he noticed
that the pilgrims were attentive and excited. When he had finished,
they turned to one another and said that this must be the prophet expected by their Jewish and hanifi neighbors. If Muhammad really
was the messenger of Allah, he might be just the person to solve the
seemingly insuperable problems of Yathrib.

Yathrib was not a city like Mecca, but a series of hamlets, each
occupied by a different tribal group, and each heavily fortified.[16] The
settlement was situated in an oasis, a fertile island of about twenty
square miles, surrounded by volcanic rocks and uncultivable stony
ground. Some of its inhabitants engaged in trade, but most were
farmers, making a living out of their dates, palm orchards, and arable
fields. Unlike the Quraysh, they were not wholly dependent upon
commerce, and had retained more of the old badawah values, including, unfortunately, an entrenched hostility to other tribal groups.
As a result, the oasis was engulfed in an escalating series of apparently unstoppable wars. The area had originally been cultivated by

pioneering Jewish settlers and by the sixth century there were about twenty Jewish tribes in Yathrib, many of whose members may have been Arabs who had assimilated to Judaism.[7] They preserved a separate religious identity, but otherwise were almost indistinguishable from their pagan neighbors. Clan and tribal loyalty came first, and there was no united "Jewish community." The Jewish tribes formed separate allegiances with Arab groups and were often at war with one another. Their date crop had made them rich, but they were also skilled jewellers, manufacturers of weapons, and craftsmen. The five largest Jewish clans—Thalabah, Hudl, Qurayzah, Nadir, and Qaynuqa', the last of which controlled the only market in Yathrib—had achieved an almost complete monopoly of the economy that they had pioneered.

But during the sixth century, the Arab tribe of the Bani Qaylah had emigrated from South Arabia and settled in the oasis, alongside the Jews. They then formed two distinct clans—Aws and Khazraj—which eventually became two separate tribes. Gradually the Arabs acquired their own land, built their own fortresses, and by the early seventh century were in a slightly stronger position than the Jews. But despite the inevitable competition over resources, Jews and pagans were able to coexist. The Jews often employed the Arabs to transport their dates, while the Arabs respected the skills and heritage of the Jews, seeing them as "a people of high lineage and properties, whereas we were but an Arab tribe, who did not possess any palm trees nor vineyards, being people of only sheep and camels."[18]

But by the time of the pilgrims' meeting with Muhammad in

620, the situation had deteriorated. The engrained tribal rivalry had surfaced, and Aws and Khazraj were now engaged in a bloody conflict with one another. The Jewish clans had become involved in their struggle, Nadir and Qurayzah supporting Aws, while Qaynuqaʿ was allied to Khazraj. By 617, there was stalemate: neither side could gain ascendancy. Everybody was exhausted by the violence. At certain key moments, ʿAbdullah ibn Ubayy, a chief of Khazraj, had stood aloof from the fighting and thus acquired a reputation for impartiality. Some saw him as a possible king or supreme chief, who could enforce law and order. But the Arabs were averse to monarchy, and this type of experiment had never worked well in the peninsula. The Aws were naturally reluctant to hand the leadership to a member of Khazraj, while the other chiefs of Khazraj were equally unwilling to relinquish their power to Ibn Ubayy.

The six pilgrims immediately realized that, as the spokesman of Allah, Muhammad would be a far more effective arbitrator (*hakam*) than Ibn Ubayy. They had no problems with his religious message, because for some time the Arabs of Yathrib had been drifting towards monotheism. The Aws and Khazraj had long felt inferior to the Jews because they had no scripture of their own, and the pilgrims were thrilled to hear that God had finally sent a prophet to the Arabs. They made their formal surrender to God on the spot, with high hopes. "We have left our people, for no tribe is so divided by hatred and rancor as they. Perhaps God will unite them through you. So let us go to them and invite them to this religion of yours; and if God unites them in it, then no man will be mightier than you."[19] But they admitted that they had little influence in the oasis, and needed to consult their chiefs and wise men. If he was to be an effective hakam, it was essential that he have wide support. They promised to report back to Muhammad in a year's time. It was a decisive moment. Circumstances had forced Muhammad to look beyond Mecca and even to entertain the extraordinary idea of abandoning his tribe to take up permanent residence with another.

While awaiting developments in Yathrib, Muhammad made some changes in his household. He needed a wife, and it was suggested that he should marry Sawdah, the cousin and sister-in-law of Suhayl, the devout pagan chief of the Qurayshan clan of Amir. She had been married to one of the Muslims who had migrated to Abyssinia in 616, but was now a widow and this was a good match for her. Abu Bakr was also anxious to forge a closer link with the Prophet, and proposed that he should marry his daughter 'A'isha, who was then six years old. 'A'isha was formally betrothed to Muhammad in a ceremony at which the little girl was not present. In later years, she recalled that the first inkling she had of her new status was when her mother explained to her that she could no longer play in the streets, but must invite her friends into the family home.

Muhammad's harem has excited a good deal of prurient and ill-natured speculation in the West, but in Arabia, where polygamy was more common than the monogamous marriage that Muhammad had enjoyed with Khadijah, it would have been commonplace. These marriages were not romantic or sexual love affairs but were undertaken largely for practical ends. Sawdah seems to have been a rather homely woman, who was past her first youth; but she could take care of Muhammad's domestic needs. Muhammad may also have hoped to win over Suhayl, who was still undecided about the revelations. There was no impropriety in Muhammad's betrothal to 'A'isha. Marriages conducted in absentia to seal an alliance were often contracted at this time between adults and minors who were even younger than 'A'isha. This practice continued in Europe well into the early modern period. There was no question of consummating the marriage until 'A'isha reached puberty, when she would have been married off like any other girl. Muhammad's marriages usually had a political aim. He was starting to establish an entirely different kind of clan, based on ideology rather than kinship, but the blood tie was still a sacred value and helped to cement this experimental community.

During the hajj of 621, the six converts from Yathrib duly returned to Mecca, bringing seven others with them. Again, they met Muhammad in the gully of 'Aqabah and, in what would become known as the Pledge of 'Aqabah, promised to worship Allah alone, to refrain from stealing, lying, and infanticide, and pledged to obey Muhammad's directives concerning social justice. In return, Muhammad promised them Paradise.[20] In this first pact, the emphasis was on religion and ethics and there was as yet no political commitment. When the pilgrims returned to Yathrib, they took with them Mus'ab ibn 'Umayr, a trusted Muslim, to instruct the people of Yathrib in their new faith.

This was a wise move. Tribal hatred was so intense in the oasis, that neither Aws nor Khazraj could bear to hear a rival leading the prayers or reciting the Qur'an, so it was important that these offices were performed by a neutral outsider. At first, the Aws were antagonistic to the faith, but gradually the power of the Qur'an broke down their reserves. One day, Saʻd ibn Muʻadh, chief of one of the leading Aws clans, was horrified to hear that Musʻab was preaching in his territory, so he dispatched his second-in-command to drive him away, who bore down on the little group, brandishing his lance, and asked the Muslim how he had the temerity to spread these lies among weak, foolish people. But instead of retaliating with jahili rage, Musʻab quietly asked him to sit down and judge for himself. The deputy agreed, stuck his lance in the ground, and, as he listened to the recitation, his face changed. "What wonderful and beautiful discourse this is!" he cried, "What does one do to enter this religion?" After he had proclaimed his faith in Allah and prostrated himself in prayer, he went back to report to his chief. Saʻd was furious, grasped his own lance, and marched off to confront Musʻab himself, only to be overwhelmed in his turn by the Qur'an. He then summoned his people and asked them to follow him; trusting his leadership implicitly, the entire clan converted en masse.[21] The news of Saʻd's dramatic about-face made a great impression on other chiefs, who began to take Musʻab more seriously.

It was not long before there were Muslims in almost every family in the oasis. In Mecca, Muhammad's preaching mission had stalled largely because the Quraysh could not believe that such an ordinary person could become the messenger of Allah. But conditions in

Yathrib were different.[22] Muhammad was no commonplace fellow, who could be seen strolling around the marketplace and eating and drinking like anybody else, but a remote, mysterious figure, whose coming was eagerly anticipated. In Mecca, Muhammad's teaching threatened to damage the cult of the Haram, which was crucial to the economy, but there was no sanctuary full of idols in Yathrib. Not everybody was enamored of the new faith, however. Ibn Ubayy naturally feared that his position was being undermined; others were still committed either to the old paganism or to the hanifiyyah, but at this stage the opposition was muted. If the new prophet really could solve the problems of Yathrib, there might be some material advantage to be gained from him. The Jewish tribes were also prepared to give Muhammad the benefit of the doubt, especially since the Muslims honored their prophets and had adopted some of their own customs.

Muhammad had recently introduced some new practices. As a result of the night journey, perhaps, Muslims now prayed facing the direction *(qiblah)* of Jerusalem, reaching out to the holy city of the People of the Book. Muhammad had also instructed Mus'ab to hold a special prayer meeting on Friday afternoon while the Jews were preparing for their Sabbath, and to fast with the Jews on Yom Kippur. Muslims would now pray in the middle of the day, as the Jews did, and observe a modified version of the Jewish dietary laws, similar to those adopted by the early Christians.[23] Scholars used to think that Muhammad introduced these new devotions in order to appeal to the Jews of Yathrib, but this view has recently been challenged. Muhammad would not have expected the Jews to convert to his religion, because they had their own revealed din. God had decreed that each community should have its own messenger.[24] But it was natural for Muslims to pray and fast in the same way as the other members of the Abrahamic family.

In 622 a large party of pilgrims left Yathrib for the hajj. Some were pagans, but seventy-three of the men and two of the women were Muslims. Yet again, Muhammad went out to greet them at 'Aqabah, but this time the meeting took place at dead of night. On this occasion, there was a sense of menace and of bridges being irrevocably burned. The Qur'an speaks of the "scheming" of the Quraysh: perhaps Muhammad had reason to believe that the kafirun were plotting to expel him and bar the Muslims from the Haram.[25] At all events, Muhammad was now taking practical steps to leave his tribe. Ibn Ishaq claims that this was a positive decision on his part, but the Qur'an repeatedly claims that the Muslims were "expelled" or "driven out" of Mecca.[26] The meeting was conducted in deadly secrecy. The Muslims from Yathrib did not even mention it to the pagans in their party, in case they gossiped and alerted the Quraysh to what was afoot.

Muhammad was about to do something absolutely unprecedented.[27] He was asking the Muslims of Mecca to make a *hijrah* (migration) to Yathrib. This did not merely involve a change of address. The Muslims were about to abandon their kinsfolk and accept the permanent protection of strangers. In Arabia, where the tribe was the most sacred value of all, this amounted to blasphemy; it was far more shocking than the Qur'anic rejection of the goddesses. There had always been a system of confederation, whereby an individual or an entire group could become honorary members of another tribe, but these were usually temporary arrangements and had never entailed alienation from one's own people. The very word *hijrah* suggests a painful severance. The root *HJR* has been translated: "he cut himself off from friendly or loving communication or inter-course . . . he ceased . . . to associate with them."[28] Henceforth the Muslims who made the *hijrah* to Yathrib would be called the *Muha-jirah*, the Emigrants: this traumatic dislocation was central to their new identity.

The Muslims of Yathrib were also embarking on a dangerous experiment. Even if a foreigner was adopted by a tribe, he always remained a *zalim* ("outsider"), a word which carried the connotation "base, ignoble, evil."[29] Poets described the zalim as a useless, super-fluous accretion. Tribal loyalty was experienced as burning love of kinsfolk and harsh contempt for the alien. Anybody who put a despised zalim before his own people invited passionate scorn and revulsion. But now the Aws and Khazraj were about to swear allegiance to the Qurayshi Muhammad, and promising to give protection and help (*nasr*) to a large group of outsiders who would inevitably put a strain on the limited resources of the oasis. Henceforth the Muslims of Yathrib would be known as the *Ansar*. This is usually translated "the Helpers," but this gives a somewhat anemic impression of what was involved. Nasr meant that you had to be ready to back up your aid with force. When they met Muhammad that night in 'Aqabah, the Helpers had decided to make a second pact with Muhammad, which would be known as the Pledge of War.

When the time came, the Ansar left their pagan companions sleeping in their tents and stole "softly like sandgrouse" to 'Aqabah, where they met Muhammad and his uncle 'Abbas, who acted as his spokesman. 'Abbas had not converted to Islam and he must have been shocked by Muhammad's decision to leave Mecca, but he wanted to make sure that he would be safe in Yathrib. Muhammad, he said, was protected by the Hashim in Mecca, but was ready to forgo this security in order to join the Ansar. If they had the smallest doubt about his safety, they should give up the entire project immediately. But the Ansar stood firm. Bara' Ibn Mar'ur, a chief of Khazraj, took Muhammad by the hand, and swore that Aws and Khazraj would both extend to Muhammad exactly the same protection as they gave to their own women and children. But while he was speaking, another Helper interrupted. What if Muhammad went back to Mecca and abandoned Yathrib to the wrath of the Quraysh? Muhammad smiled and replied: "I am of you and you are of me. I will war against them that war against you and be at peace with those at peace with you."[30] And so the Ansar made this solemn oath: "We pledged ourselves to war in complete obedience to the apostle, in weal or woe, in ease and hardship and evil circumstances; that we would not wrong anyone; that we would speak the truth at all times;

and that in God's service we would fear the censure of none."[31]

The pact was couched in tribal terminology, and concentrated on mutual defense.[32] There was as yet no thought of a single, united ummah. Aws, Khazraj, and Quraysh would still operate separately. Muhammad would not go to Yathrib as head of state, but simply as the arbitrator (hakam) of disputes between Aws and Khazraj and as the chief of the Emigrants from Mecca. The Ansar would be ruled by twelve "overseers" from the various clans. Even though Islam had made great strides in Yathrib—after a single year, the Muslim community there was almost as large as the beleaguered ummah in Mecca—the fact remained that even after the hijrah, the Muslims would remain a tiny minority in the oasis, dwarfed in size by the aloof, appraising pagans, hanifs, and Jews.[33] The Pledge of War marked a major expansion of Islam: the new religion had spread to other tribal groups, but it had not yet transcended the tribal ethos. The hijrah was a risky enterprise, an irrevocable, frightening step. Nobody knew how it would work out, because nothing quite like it had ever happened in Arabia before.

After the hajj, the Ansar returned to Yathrib to await the arrival of the Muslim fugitives. The Qur'an now adopted the Aramaic name that the Jews gave to the settlement of Yathrib: *medinta* ("the city"). Yathrib was about to become *al-Madinat*, the city of the Prophet. In Mecca, Muhammad began to persuade Muslims to make the hijrah, but he did not command it. Anybody who felt it to be beyond his or her strength was free to remain behind. But during July and August 622, about seventy Muslims set off with their families to Medina, where they were lodged in the houses of the Ansar until they could set up their own homes. The Quraysh do not seem to have made a concerted effort to detain them though some women and children were forcibly prevented from leaving, and one man was carted back in triumph, tied to his camel. For their part, the Muslims were careful not to draw attention to their flight, and usually agreed to meet up outside the city limits and to travel in small, unobtrusive groups. 'Umar left with his family; 'Uthman ibn 'Affan and Ruqayyah made the journey with Zayd and Hamzah, but Muhammad and Abu Bakr stayed behind until nearly everybody had left. But it was not long before this major defection left disturbing gaps in the city, revealing the open wound that Muhammad had inflicted on his tribe. The big houses in the middle of Mecca looked desolate and portentous to passers by, "doors blowing to and fro, empty of inhabitants."[34]

In August, shortly before he was due to leave, Mu'tim, Muhammad's Meccan protector, died. Muhammad's position in Mecca was now untenable, because he was fair game for assassination. There was a special meeting to discuss his fate in the assembly, from which Abu Lahab pointedly absented himself. Some of the elders simply wanted to throw Muhammad out of Mecca, but they were overruled by those who felt that to allow him to join those unprincipled renegades in Yathrib would be dangerous. Abu Jahl came up with a plan: each clan would select a strong and well-protected young man. Collectively, they would represent the entire tribe, and would kill Muhammad together. There would be no vendetta, because the Hashim could not take on the whole of Quraysh.

So that night a band of carefully chosen youths gathered outside Muhammad's home, but were disturbed to hear the voices of Sawdah and some of the Prophet's daughters through the window. It would be shameful to kill a man in the presence of his women, so they decided to wait until he left the house the following morning. One of them peered in and saw a figure lying in bed, wrapped in Muhammad's cloak. Unbeknownst to them, Muhammad had already escaped through a back window, leaving 'Ali lying apparently asleep, wearing his clothes. When 'Ali strolled outside the next morning, the young men realized that they had been tricked, and the Quraysh offered a reward of a hundred camel mares to anybody who would bring Muhammad back, dead or alive.

By this time, Muhammad and Abu Bakr were hiding in a mountain cave just outside the city. They stayed there for three days, and from time to time, their supporters slipped out to bring them news and provisions. At one point, it was said, a search party actually passed the cave, but did not bother to look inside because an enormous spider's web covered the entrance and a rock dove, who had clearly been sitting on her eggs for some time, had her nest in an acacia tree in exactly the place where a man would have to put his foot when climbing into the cave. All the while, Muhammad experienced a deep calm and a strong sense of God's presence. The Qur'an recalls how he comforted Abu Bakr: " 'grieve not: verily God is with us.' And thereupon God bestowed upon him from on high His [gift of] inner peace."[35] Increasingly the

Qur'an would insist that when Muslims found themselves in frightening or disturbing circumstances, they should be serene and tranquil, and should never fall prey to the impetuous rage and vengeful fury of jahiliyyah.

When the hue and cry had died down, Muhammad and Abu Bakr climbed out of the cave, taking care not to disturb the rock dove, and mounted the two camels that Abu Bakr had prepared for their journey. Abu Bakr wanted to give the better camel to Muhammad, but he insisted on paying for her. This was his personal hijrah, his sacrifice to Allah, and it was important to make the whole event entirely his own. Muhammad called the camel mare Qaswa', and she remained his favorite mount for the rest of his life. It was a dangerous trip, because while he was on the road, Muhammad did not enjoy anybody's protection, so their guide took them by a circuitous route, and they zigzagged back and forth to throw any pursuers off the scent.

In the meantime, the Muslims were anxiously awaiting their arrival in Medina. Several of the Emigrants from Mecca were living in Quba', the southernmost point of the oasis, and every day after morning prayers they used to climb the volcanic rocks and scan the barren terrain outside the settlement. On the morning of September 4, 622, one of the Jews spotted a cloud of dust on the horizon and called out to the Ansar: "Sons of Qaylah! He is come! He is come!" At once men, women, and children surged out to meet the travellers and found them resting under a palm tree.

Muhammad and Abu Bakr stayed in Quba' for three days, but

the Muslims in the "city" (as the most densely populated part of the oasis was called) were impatient to see him, so he set off to meet them and decide where he was going to live. Along the way, several people begged him to alight and make his home with them, but Muhammad courteously refused because he was anxious to remain independent of the warring groups within Medina. Instead, he gave Qaswa' her head, and asked God to guide her. Eventually, she fell to her knees outside a *mirbad*, a place for drying dates, which belonged to one of the Ansar. Muhammad got down, allowed his luggage to be carried into the nearest house and then began to negotiate with the owner for the sale of the land. Once the price was agreed upon, all the Muslims got to work to build the Prophet's residence, which would also serve as a place for prayer. This was hard for the Emigrants, because the Quraysh were not used to manual labor, and the stylish 'Uthman found the work particularly grueling.

The first Muslim building was not imposing but it became the model for all future mosques. It was primarily a masjid, "a place of prostration," an open space roomy enough for the entire community to perform the salat together, and it expressed the austerity of the early Islamic ideal. The roof was supported by tree trunks, and there was no elaborate pulpit; Muhammad stood on a simple stool to address the congregation. Muhammad and his wives lived in little huts round the edge of the big courtyard in front of the mosque. This was a place for public and political meetings; the poor of Medina were also invited to congregate there for alms, food and care.

This humble building in Medina expressed the ideal of tawhid.[36] Muhammad wanted to show that the sexual, the sacred, and the domestic could—and, indeed, must—be integrated. Similarly politics, welfare, and the ordering of social life must be brought into the ambit of holiness. In housing his wives within a stone's throw of the mosque, Muhammad was tacitly proclaiming that there must be no distinction between public and private life, and no discrimination between the sexes. Holiness in Islam was inclusive rather than exclusive. If they wished, Jews and Christians could worship in the mosque, because they too were part of God's family.

The building was completed in April, 623, about seven months after the hijrah. In the northern wall, a stone marked the qiblah, the direction of prayer, orienting the people towards Jerusalem. At first there was no official summons to salat, but this was obviously unsatisfactory, as everybody came at different times. Muhammad thought of using a ram's horn, like the Jews, or a wooden clapper, like the local Christians, but one of the Emigrants had an important dream. A man, clad in a green cloak, had told him that somebody with a loud, resonant voice should announce the service, crying *Allahu Akhbar* ("God is greater") as a reminder of a Muslim's first priority. Muhammad liked the idea and Bilal, the former Abyssinian slave with the big voice, was an obvious choice. Every morning he climbed to the top of the tallest house in the vicinity of the mosque, and sat on the rooftop waiting for dawn. Then he would stretch out his arms, and before beginning the call, would pray: "O God, I praise Thee and ask Thy help for Quraysh that they may accept Thy religion."[37] The Muslims may have changed their qiblah to Jerusalem, but they had not forgotten Mecca. When Muhammad learned that many of the Emigrants were deeply homesick, he prayed: "Lord, make us love this town as much as you made us love Mecca, and even more so."[38]

The immense uprooting of the hijrah meant that even though they still used the old tribal terminology, the Muslims had to create an entirely different type of community. One of the first things Muhammad did was set up a system of "brothering" whereby each Meccan was assigned an Ansar "brother" to help Muslims to bond across the lines of kinship. The political separation of Emigrants and Helpers was soon dropped: when the first of the twelve Ansari "overseers" died, Muhammad simply took over his position.[39] The Muslims were gradually creating a "neo-tribe," which interpreted the old kinship relationships differently. Those who had made the hijrah were to regard themselves as distinct from the Muslims who had remained behind in Mecca, even though they all belonged to the same blood group. Whatever their tribe or clan, Muslims must never fight one another. Emigrants and Helpers must become as solidly united as any conventional tribe.[40] Like the tribe, the ummah was "one community to the exclusion of all men," and would make "confederates" of non-Muslim allies in the usual way.[41]

As chieftain of the ummah, Muhammad could now implement his moral and social reforms in a way that had been impossible in Mecca. His goal was to create a society of hilm. Those who kept the faith (*mu'min*) were not simply "believers." Their faith must be expressed in practical actions: they must pray, share their wealth, and in matters that concerned the community, "consult among themselves" to preserve the unity of the ummah. If attacked, they could defend themselves, but instead of lashing out in the old, uncontrolled jahili way, they must always be prepared to forgive an injury. Automatic, vengeful retaliation—the cardinal duty of muruwah—could be a great evil. "Hence, whoever pardons [his foe] and makes peace, his reward rests with God," the Qur'an insisted tirelessly. "If one is patient in adversity and forgives—this, behold, is indeed something to set one's heart upon."[42]

But this transformation could not be achieved overnight, because the old spirit of jahiliyyah still lurked in Muslim hearts. Shortly after the hijrah, one of the pagan Arabs noticed a crowd of Muslims, which included members of both Aws and Khazraj, chatting together amicably as though their tribes had never been sworn enemies. He was furious. Clearly Islam was making them soft and feeble! He ordered a young Jewish man to sit near the group and recite poems that reminded them of the old bitter feuds. It was not long before the engrained tribal chauvinism flared up, and the Muslims were soon at one another's throats. Muhammad hurried to the scene in great distress. "Are you still tempted by the call of jahiliyyah when I am here among you?" he demanded, "when God has guided you . . . honored you, and cut off thereby the bond of jahiliyyah from you, delivered you from a state of defiant ingratitude (*kufr*), and made you friends of each other?" Deeply ashamed, the Ansar wept and embraced.[43]

Not all the Muslims of Medina were committed to change. Some had embraced Islam purely for material gain, and they were sitting on the fence, waiting to see how this new venture would turn out. The Qur'an called these people the "waverers" or the "Hypocrites," (*munafiqun*) because they were not sincere and kept changing their minds.[44] When they were with devout Muslims, they cried: "We believe [as you believe]," but in the company of other doubters, they assured them: "Verily, we are with you; we were only mocking!"[45] Their leader was Ibn Ubayy, who had become a Muslim but remained resentful and critical of the new faith. Muhammad always behaved respectfully to him, and allowed him to address the community every week during the Friday prayers, but from time to time his buried hostility came to the surface. "Don't be hard on him," one of the Helpers begged Muhammad after a particularly unpleasant incident, "for before God sent you to us we were making a diadem to crown him, and by God, he thinks you have robbed him of a kingdom."[46]

Some of the Jews were also becoming hostile to the newcomers. Muhammad did not expect them to convert to Islam, and their quarrel with him was not primarily religious but political and economic. The Jews' position in the oasis had deteriorated, and if Muhammad succeeded in uniting Aws and Khazraj, they would have no chance of regaining their former supremacy. Hence three of the larger Jewish tribes thought it wiser to support Ibn Ubbay and the pagan Arabs in the oasis who remained opposed to Muhammad.[47] The early Muslim historians tell us that they mounted a scholarly polemic against the theology of the Qur'an, but this probably reflected Jewish-Muslim debate during the eighth and ninth centuries.[48] The Jews of seventh century Medina had only a limited knowledge of Torah and Talmud, were not strictly observant, and most were used to seeing their faith as a variant of Arabian religion.[49] The idea of an Arabian prophet was not a strange idea to them: they had a prophet of their own called Ibn Sayyad, who, like Muhammad, wrapped himself in a cloak, recited inspired verses, and claimed to be the apostle of God.[50]

But if there were no learned rabbinical debates, the Muslims probably encountered a good deal of populist religious chauvinism in Medina. Ibn Ishaq tells us that when they came to the mosque, some of the Jews would "laugh and scoff" at the Qur'an.[51] Many Jews were friendly and Muhammad probably learned a great deal from them, but some of the People of the Book had ideas that he found very strange indeed. The idea of an exclusive religion was alien to Muhammad; he hated sectarian quarrels,[52] and was offended by the idea of a "chosen people" or the conviction that only Jews or Christians could get to Paradise.[53] He was also bewildered to learn that some Christians believed that God was a trinity and that Jesus was the son of Allah.[54] But he remained convinced that these peculiar notions were the heretical deviations of a deluded minority.[55] The Qur'an reminded Muslims that many of the People of the Book were "upright people," who recite God's messages throughout the night and prostrate themselves [before him]. They believe in God and the Last Day, and enjoin the doing of what is right and forbid the doing of what is wrong, and vie with one another in doing God's works; and these are among the righteous.[56]

Muslims must remember that every community had its own specially revealed din, so they must not take part in these pointless squabbles; if the People of the Book attacked their faith, Muslims must behave with hilm, and courteously reply: "God knows best what you are doing."[57]

To avoid this sterile controversy, Muhammad, like the hanifs, decided to return to the "religion of Abraham," who was neither a "Jew" nor a "Christian," because he had lived long before either the Torah or the Gospel.[58] After the hijrah, the Qur'an started to apply the words "hanif" and "hanifiyyah" to the Muslims and Islam, but gave them a new interpretation. For Muhammad, hanifiyyah simply meant total submission to God; this had been the original, unadulterated message of the prophets, before it had been corrupted by sectarian chauvinism. Abraham, for example, had not belonged to an exclusive cult. He had simply been a muslim, "one who surrendered himself" and a "man of pure faith" (hanif).[59] When Abraham and Ishmael had rebuilt the Kabah together, they had not developed an exclusive theology, but had simply wanted to give their lives entirely to Allah. "O our Sustainer!" they had prayed, "Make us surrender ourselves unto Thee, and show us our ways of worship." Muslims had been driven out of Mecca because of religious intolerance, so they must avoid all exclusivity.[60] Instead of stridently insisting that they alone had the monopoly of truth, the true Muslims merely said: "Behold, my prayer, and [all] my acts of worship and my living and my dying are for God [alone], the Sustainer of all the worlds."[61] It was idolatry to take pride in belonging to a particular religious tradition rather than concentrating upon Allah himself.

Towards the end of January 624, Muhammad received a revelation while he was leading the Friday prayers, and made the congregation turn around and pray in the direction of Mecca instead of Jerusalem. They would now face the house built by Abraham, the man of pure faith.

> We have seen thee [O Prophet] often turn thy face towards heaven [for guidance], and now We shall indeed make thee turn too in prayer in a direction which will fulfil thy desire. Turn then thy face towards the Inviolable House of Worship; and wherever you all may be, turn your faces towards it [in prayer].[62]

It was a reminder that they were not following any of the established religions, but God himself. It was a declaration of independence. Muslims need no longer feel that they were following lamely in the footsteps of the older faiths. "Hold them not in awe," God said, "but stand in awe of me and [obey me]."[63] The new qiblah delighted both the Emigrants and the Helpers, and would bind them more closely together. They all loved the Kabah, which was more deeply rooted in Arab tradition than the distant city of Jerusalem. But there was a problem. The Kabah was in Mecca, and relations with the Quraysh had recently become more strained than ever before.

Chapter Four

Jihad

THE CHANGE OF QIBLAH had occurred at the end of a period of uncertainty. Muhammad and the community had been restlessly "turning this way and that," searching for guidance in their confusion. Muhammad knew that a prophet had to make a difference to the world. He could not simply withdraw from the mainstream. He had to put God's revealed will into practice and create a just, egalitarian society. But the hijrah had pushed the Muslims into a peripheral and anomalous position. Even though Muhammad had begun to implement his social reforms, he knew that he would make no lasting impression on Arabia as long as he was confined to and isolated in Medina. Mecca, the "mother of cities," was crucial to the development of the peninsula. Arabia needed the commercial genius of the Quraysh. Mecca was now the center of the Muslim world. They yearned towards it in prayer several times a day, but it was coming to seem like an absent, inaccessible lover.[1] Muslims could not even make the hajj, like other Arabs. Muhammad realized that Mecca was the key to his mission. The hostility of the Quraysh had eradicated the ummah from the tribal map and pushed it into a political limbo. Without Mecca, Islam was doomed to marginality. Somehow Muhammad would have to make peace with his people. But after the first shock of the hijrah, most of the Quraysh seemed to have forgotten all about the Muslims. Before Muhammad could seek reconciliation with Mecca, he had to make the Quraysh take notice of him.

He also had to secure his position in Medina. He knew that, as far as most of the Medinese were concerned, he was still on trial. They had defied the might of the Quraysh by taking the migrants in because they expected some material advantage, and here too, Muhammad had to deliver. At the very least, he had to ensure that the Emigrants did not become a drain upon the economy. But it was difficult for them to earn a living. Most of them were merchants or bankers, but there was very little opportunity for trade in Medina, where the wealthier Arab and Jewish tribes had achieved a monopoly. The Emigrants had no experience of farming, and in any case all the available land had already been taken. They would become a burden to the Helpers, unless they found an independent source of income, and there was one obvious way to achieve this.

Medina was well placed to attack the Meccan caravans on their way to and from Syria, and shortly after Muhammad had arrived in Medina, he had started to send bands of Emigrants on raiding expeditions.[2] Their aim was not to shed blood, but to secure an income

by capturing camels, merchandise, and prisoners, who could be held
for ransom. Nobody would have been particularly shocked by this
development. The ghazu was a normal expedient in times of hardship, though some of the Arabs would have been surprised by the
Muslims' temerity in taking on the mighty Quraysh, especially as
they were clearly inexperienced warriors. During the first two years
after the hijrah, Muhammad dispatched eight of these expeditions.
He did not usually go himself but commissioned people such as
Hamzah and 'Ubaydah ibn al-Harith, but it was difficult to get ac-
curate information about the caravans' itinerary, and none of these
early raids was successful.

The Quraysh were not a warlike people. They had left the
nomadic life behind long ago and had lost both the habit and
skill of the ghazu; the Qur'an shows that some of the Emigrants
found the very idea of fighting distasteful.[3] But Muhammad was
not discouraged. Even though the Emigrants desperately needed
an income, plunder was not his primary objective. The raiders
may have come back empty handed, but they had at least brought
the Muslims to the attention of Mecca. The Quraysh were
rattled. They had to take precautions that had never been necessary
before. Merchants complained that they felt more vulnerable;
they had to make inconvenient detours and the flow of trade
in and out of Mecca was slightly disrupted. In September 623,
Muhammad himself led a ghazu against a large caravan led by
Ummayah ibn Khalaf; the spoils looked so promising that a record
200 Muslims volunteered for the expedition. But yet again the

caravan eluded the raiders and there was no fighting.

In the steppes, the ghazu needed no theoretical justification; it was seen as an unavoidable necessity in time of scarcity. But Muhammad had been determined to transcend the old tribal norms. The Qur'an had instructed Muslims to say "Peace be with you!" to the kafirun, not attack them while they were going about their business. Shortly after Muhammad arrived in Medina, he received a revelation that took a more militant line.

> Permission [to fight] is given to those against whom war is being wrongfully waged—and, verily, God has indeed the power to succor them—those who have been driven from their homelands against all right for no other reason than their saying "Our Sustainer is God!"
>
> For if God had not enabled people to defend themselves against one another, [all] monasteries and churches and synagogues and mosques—in [all of] which God's name is abundantly extolled—would surely have been destroyed [ere now].[4]

The Qur'an had begun to develop a primitive just war theory. In the steppes, aggressive warfare was praiseworthy; but in the Qur'an, self-defense was the only possible justification for hostilities and the preemptive strike was condemned.[5] War was always a terrible evil, but it was sometimes necessary in order to preserve decent values, such as freedom of worship. Even here, the Qur'an did not abandon its pluralism: synagogues and churches as well as mosques should be protected. The Muslims felt that they had suffered a fearful assault; their expulsion from Mecca was an act that had no justification. Exile from the tribe violated the deepest sanction of Arabia; it had attacked the core of the Muslims' identity.

But Muhammad had embarked upon a dangerous course. He was living in a chronically violent society and he saw these raids not simply as a means of bringing in much-needed income, but as a way of resolving his quarrel with the Quraysh. We have discovered in our own day, that waging war for the sake of peace is a high-risk venture. The ruthlessness of battle can lead to actions that flout the very principles that the warriors are fighting for, so that in the end neither side can claim the high moral ground. Muhammad tried to give his ghazu ethical grounding but he had no experience of a long military campaign, and would learn that, once it has started, a cycle of violence achieves an independent momentum, and can spin tragically out of control.

At first, Muhammad fought according to the traditional rules, but in January 624, just before the change of the qiblah, he had his first experience of the unpredictability of warfare.[6] The Emigrants were becoming more confident. During the winter months, the Quraysh sent their caravans south, so they no longer had to pass Medina. But ever anxious to attract their attention, Muhammad sent a small raiding party of nine men to attack one of these southbound caravans. It was the end of Rajab, one of the "sacred months" when all fighting was forbidden. On the last day of Rajab, the Muslims came upon a small caravan encamped in Nakhlah. What should they do? If they waited until the following day, when the truce ended, the caravan would be able to return unscathed to Mecca. They decided to attack. The first arrow killed one of the merchants, most of the others fled, but the Muslims took two prisoners whom they brought back to Medina with the captured merchandise.

But instead of greeting the raiders as conquering heroes, the Muslims were horrified to hear that the raid had violated the sacred month. For a few days, Muhammad did not know how to respond. He had, after all, abandoned much Meccan religion and may have imagined that he could jettison the forbidden months too. The raid had been a success. Not only were there rich pickings, but he had shown the Quraysh that he could attack them almost on their own doorstep. He had also impressed many of the Medinese. But there was something dubious about the whole business. Muhammad had never condemned the practice of the forbidden months before; the sources seem uneasy about the incident. Muhammad had discovered that however idealistic your war might be at the outset, something distasteful is likely to occur sooner rather than later.

Eventually Muhammad received a new revelation that reiterated the central principle of his just war. Yes, it had been wrong to break the sacred truce, but the policy of the Quraysh in driving the Muslims from their homes had been even more heinous. "They will not cease to fight against you till they have turned you away from your faith," the Qur'an warned Muhammad. As to fighting during the forbidden month, this was indeed an "awesome thing,"

But turning men away from the path of God and denying Him and [turning them away from] the Inviolable House of Worship and expelling its people therefrom—[all this] is far more awesome in the sight of God, since oppression is more awesome than killing.[7]

Muhammad, therefore, accepted the booty and reassured the community; he divided the spoils equally among the Emigrants and began negotiations with the Quraysh for an exchange of prisoners: he would trade the Meccan captives for two Muslims still living in Mecca who wanted to make the hijrah. But one of the prisoners was so impressed by what he saw in Medina that he decided to remain and convert to Islam. The incident is a good example of the way Muhammad was beginning to work. In his novel position, he could not rely on customary procedure. He was feeling his way forward step by step, responding to events as they unfolded. He had no fixed master plan and, unlike some of his more impetuous companions, he rarely responded to a crisis immediately but took time to reflect until finally—sometimes pale and sweating with the effort—he would bring forth what seemed an inspired solution.

A few weeks later, during the month of Ramadan (March 624), Muhammad led a large Muslim contingent to intercept a Meccan caravan that Abu Sufyan was bringing back from Syria.[8] This was one of the most important caravans of the year and, encouraged by the success of Nakhlah, a large contingent of Helpers volunteered to join the raid. About 314 Muslims set out from Medina and rode to the well of Badr, near the Red Sea coast, where they hoped to ambush the caravan. This expedition would be one of the most formative events in the early history of Islam, but at the outset it seemed just another ghazu and several of the most committed Muslims stayed at home, including 'Uthman ibn 'Affan, whose wife Ruqayyah, the Prophet's daughter, was dangerously ill.

At first it looked as though the caravan would, as usual, escape. Abu Sufyan got wind of the Muslims' plan and instead of taking his usual route across the Hijaz, he turned sharply away from the coast and dispatched a local tribesman to Mecca to get help. The Quraysh were incensed at Muhammad's insolence, which they regarded as a slur on their honor, and all the leading men were determined to rescue the caravan. Abu Jahl, of course, was eager for the fray. The obese Ummayah ibn Khalaf was crammed into his armor, and even members of Muhammad's own family rode out against him, convinced that this time he had gone too far. Abu Lahab was sick, but two of Abu Talib's sons, his uncle 'Abbas, and Khadijah's nephew Hakim joined the thousand men who rode out of Mecca that night and took the road to Badr.

In the meantime, Abu Sufyan had managed to elude the Muslims and taken the caravan beyond their reach. He sent word that the merchandise was safe and that the army should turn back. The sources make it clear that when it came to the point many of the Quraysh were reluctant to fight their kinsmen. But Abu Jahl would have none of this. "By Allah!" he cried. "We will not go back until we have been to Badr. We will spend three days there, slaughter camels, and feast and drink wine; and the girls shall play for us. The Arabs will hear that we have come and will respect us in the future."[9] But these defiant words showed that even Abu Jahl did not expect a battle. He had little conception of the horror of war, which he seemed to envisage as a kind of party, complete with dancing girls. The Quraysh were so far removed from the steppes that warfare had become a chivalric sport that would enhance the prestige of Mecca.

There was a very different spirit in the Muslim camp. After the trauma and terror of the hijrah, the Emigrants could not view the situation in such a confident, carefree light. As soon as Muhammad heard that the Meccan army was approaching, he consulted the other chiefs. The Muslims were vastly outnumbered. They had expected an ordinary ghazu, not a full-scale battle, which was a very different matter. Muhammad was not the commander-in-chief; he could not command obedience, but the men decided to fight it out. As Sa'd ibn Mu'adh said on behalf of the Helpers:

> We have given you our word and agreement to hear and obey; so go where you wish and we are with you, and by God, if you were to ask us to cross this sea and you plunged into it, we would plunge into it with you. We do not dislike the idea of meeting your enemy tomorrow. We are experienced in war, trustworthy in combat.[10]

Unlike the Quraysh, the Aws and Khazraj were practiced soldiers, after years of tribal warfare in Yathrib. But even so, the odds were overwhelmingly against them and all the Muslims hoped that they would not have to fight.

For two days, the two armies gazed bleakly at one another from opposite ends of the valley. The Quraysh looked impressive in their white tunics and glittering armor and despite Sa'd's stirring words, some of the Muslims wanted to retreat. There was great fear in the camp. The Prophet tried to rouse their spirits. He told them that in a dream God had promised to send a thousand angels to fight alongside them.[11] But while the Quraysh were feasting and drinking, certain that the Muslims would surrender, Muhammad was making practical preparations. He lined up his troops in close formation and positioned his men by the wells, depriving the Quraysh of water and forcing them, when the time came, to advance uphill, fighting with the sun in their eyes. But when he looked at the huge Meccan army, he wept. "O Allah," he prayed, "If this band that is with me perishes, there will be no one after me to worship You; all the believers will abandon the true religion."[12] He realized that this battle would be decisive. If the Muslims allowed the Quraysh to force them back to Medina, the ummah would make no lasting impact on Arabia. Something of his determined resolve must have been conveyed to his men. The Qur'an describes the great peace that descended upon the soldiers at this frightening moment. There was a sudden rainstorm, which seemed a good omen.[13]

Meanwhile the Quraysh had become more alarmed. The chiefs had dispatched a spy to report on the enemy troops. He was aghast to see the grim resolution on the faces of the Muslims and begged the Quraysh not to fight. He had "seen camels carrying Death—the camels of Yathrib laden with certain death." Not one of the Muslims would die before he had killed at least one of the Meccans, and, the spy concluded despairingly, how could the Quraysh live with themselves after that? They would constantly be looking into the face of a neighbor who had killed one of their kinsfolk. But Abu Jahl was beyond reason and accused him of cowardice—a jibe that no Arab could ignore. He then turned to the brother of the man slain by the Muslim raiders at Nakhlah, who emitted a savage war cry. Immediately, said Ibn Ishaq, "war was kindled and all was marred and the folk held stubbornly to their evil course."[14] The Quraysh began to advance slowly over the sand dunes. Observing the command of the Qur'an, Muhammad refused to strike first, and even after the battle commenced, he seemed reluctant to unleash his men until Abu Bakr told him to leave his prayers and engage his troops, because God would certainly give them victory.

In the fierce skirmish that followed, the Quraysh soon found that they were getting the worst of it. They fought with careless bravado, as though this was a knightly tournament, and had no concerted strategy. But the Muslims did have a disciplined plan. They began by bombarding the enemy with arrows, drawing their swords for hand-to-hand combat only at the last minute. By midday, the Quraysh had fled in disarray, leaving some fifty of their leading men, including Abu Jahl himself, dead on the field. There were only fourteen Muslim casualties.

Jubilantly, the Muslims began to round up the prisoners and

draw their swords. In tribal warfare, there was no quarter for the vanquished. Casualties were mutilated and captives were either slain or tortured. Muhammad immediately ordered his troops to desist. A revelation came down to ensure that the prisoners of war must either be released or ransomed.[15] Even in war, Muslims would abjure the savage customs of the past.

Constantly the Qur'an insists upon the importance of mercy and forgiveness, even during armed conflict.[16] While engaged in hostilities, Muslims must fight with courage and steadfastness in order to bring the conflict to an end as quickly as possible. But the moment the enemy asks for peace, Muslims must lay down their arms.[17] They must accept any offer of truce, whatever conditions are imposed, even if they suspect the enemy of double-dealing. And although it is important to fight persecution and oppression, the Qur'an constantly reminds Muslims that it is much better to sit down and solve the problem by courteous discussion.[18] True, God permitted retaliation in the Torah—eye for eye, tooth for tooth—"but he who shall forgo it out of charity will atone better for some of his past sins."[19] Retaliation would be strictly confined to those who had actually perpetrated the atrocity, a great advance on the law of vendetta, which permitted revenge against any member of the killer's tribe. The Qur'an reminded the Muslims that they were not fighting the whole tribe of Quraysh; those who had remained neutral throughout the conflict and those Muslims who had chosen to remain in Mecca must not be attacked or injured in any way.[20]

Muhammad was not a pacifist. He believed that warfare was sometimes inevitable and even necessary. After the battle of Badr, the Muslims knew that it was only a matter of time before Mecca took her revenge, and they dedicated themselves to a long, gruelling *jihad.* But the primary meaning of that word, which we hear so often today, is not "holy war" but the "effort" or "struggle" necessary to put the will of God into practice. Muslims are exhorted to strive in this endeavor on all fronts: intellectual, social, economic, spiritual, and domestic. Sometimes they would have to fight, but this was not their chief duty. On their way home from Badr, Muhammad uttered an important and oft-quoted maxim: "We are returning from the Lesser Jihad (the battle) and going to the Greater Jihad,"—the immeasurably more important and difficult struggle to reform their own society and their own hearts.

Badr had given Muhammad a far higher profile in the oasis. As they prepared for the inevitable Qurayshan riposte, a covenant was drawn up between the Prophet and the Arab and Jewish tribes of Medina, who agreed to live peaceably beside the Muslims and promised not to make a separate treaty with Mecca. All the inhabitants were required to defend the oasis against attack. The new constitution was careful to guarantee the religious freedom of the Jewish clans, but expected them to provide aid to "whosoever wars against the people of this document."[21] Muhammad needed to know who was on his side and some of those who were unwilling to accept the terms of this treaty left the oasis. They included several of the hanifs, whose devotion to the Kabah required them to remain loyal to the

Quraysh. Muhammad was still a controversial figure, but as a result of his victory at Badr, some of the Bedouin tribes were willing to become allies of Medina in the forthcoming struggle.

There were also changes in Muhammad's family life. On his return from Badr, he learned that his daughter Ruqayyah had died. 'Uthman was sincerely grieved, but was glad to accept the hand of his late wife's sister Umm Kulthum and retain his close relationship with the Prophet. One of the prisoners of war was Muhammad's pagan son-in-law, Abu l-'As, who had remained true to the traditional faith. His wife Zaynab, who was still living in Mecca, sent the ransom money to Medina together with a silver bracelet that had belonged to Khadijah. Muhammad recognized it at once and became momentarily distraught with sorrow. He let Abu l-'As go free without taking the ransom, hoping that this would encourage him to accept Islam. He refused conversion but sadly agreed to the Prophet's request that he send Zaynab and their little daughter Umamah to him in Medina, because life would now be impossible for them in Mecca. It was also time for Muhammad's youngest daughter, Fatimah, to be married, and Muhammad gave her to 'Ali. The couple set up house near the mosque.

Muhammad also took a new wife: 'Umar's daughter Hafsah, who had been recently widowed. She was beautiful and accomplished, and at the time of her marriage to the Prophet was about eighteen years old. Like her father, she could read and write, but she also had 'Umar's quick temper. 'A'isha was happy to welcome her into the household. 'A'isha would be jealous of Muhammad's other wives, but the growing bond between their fathers made these two girls firm friends. They particularly enjoyed ganging up together against the stolid, unimaginative Sawdah.

'A'isha may by this time have moved into the apartment that had been prepared for her in the mosque, though Tabari says that because of her youth she was allowed to remain for a while longer in her parents' house. Muhammad was an indulgent husband. He insisted that his wives live frugally in their tiny, sparse huts, but he always helped them with the household chores and looked after his own personal needs, mending and patching his clothes, cobbling his shoes, and tending the family goats. With 'A'isha particularly he was able to unwind, challenging her to footraces and the like. She had a sharp tongue and was by no means a shy or submissive wife, but she liked to spoil Muhammad, anointing his hair with his favorite perfume, and drinking from the same cup. One day, while they were sitting together, the Prophet busily repairing his sandals, she saw his face light up at a passing thought. Watching him for a moment, she complimented him on his bright, happy expression, and Muhammad got up and kissed her forehead, saying "Oh 'A'isha, may Allah reward you well. I am not the source of joy to you that you are to me."[22]

Muhammad lived cheek by jowl with his family and companions and saw no opposition between his public and private life.[23] It was possible for his wives to hear every word that was spoken in the mosque from their apartments. The Emigrants had immediately noticed that the women of Medina were different, less rigorously controlled than in Mecca, and soon found that their own wives were picking up the free and easy ways of the Medinese women: 'Umar was furious when his wife started to answer him back instead of meekly accepting his reproaches, and when he rebuked her she simply replied that the Prophet allowed his wives to argue with him.[24] Trouble was brewing. Muhammad's deliberate conflation of private and public was a blow to male supremacy, which can only exist if this distinction is maintained.

After the euphoria of victory had faded, Muhammad found that even though his prestige had increased in Arabia as a whole, the fear of an imminent Meccan attack was swelling the opposition party in Medina. Ibn Ubayy and his supporters were backed by three of the largest Jewish tribes—Nadir, Qurayzah and Qaynuqa'—who depended upon their commercial links with the Quraysh and wanted no part in any war against Mecca. A third column was opening up in the oasis. About ten weeks after Badr, Abu Sufyan led a token ghazu of two hundred men to the fields outside Medina, and under cover of night slipped into the territory of Nadir, where he was entertained by its chief, Sallam ibn Mishkan, who, according to Ibn Ishaq, "gave him secret information about the Muslims."[25]

Muhammad's scouts kept him informed of these developments. These three Jewish tribes were clearly a security risk. They had large armies and were experienced soldiers. If a Meccan army were to camp south of Medina, where Nadir and Qurayzah had their territories, it would be easy for them to join forces with the Quraysh and breach the city's defences. If the Quraysh decided to attack from the north, which would be their best option, Nadir and Qurayzah could attack the Muslims from the south. But a more urgent concern was Qaynuqa', the wealthiest of the Jewish tribes and former allies of Ibn Ubayy, who controlled the market in the center of Medina.[26] The Muslims had established a little market of their own, and for religious reasons did not charge interest. Taking this as a direct challenge, the Qaynuqa' decided to break their agreement with the Prophet and join the opposition. Muhammad visited their district and asked them, in the name of their common religion, to keep the peace. They listened in mutinous silence and then replied:

> O Muhammad, you seem to think that we are your people. Do not deceive yourself, because you have encountered a tribe [at Badr] with no knowledge of war and got the better of them; for by Allah, if we fight you, you will find that we are real men![27]

Muhammad withdrew and grimly awaited developments.

A few days later fighting broke out in the market of Qaynuqa', when one of the Jewish goldsmiths insulted a Muslim woman. As the hakam, Muhammad was called in to arbitrate, but the chiefs of Qaynuqa' refused to accept his judgment, barricaded themselves into their fortress and called upon their Arab allies for aid. Qaynuqa' had an army of seven hundred men, and had their allies responded, they would certainly have defeated and probably eliminated the ummah.

But the Arabs remained staunchly behind the Prophet, and Ibn Ubayy found that he was powerless to help his old confederates. After a siege of two weeks, the Qaynuqa' were forced to surrender unconditionally. Muhammad would have been expected to massacre the men and sell the women and children into slavery—the traditional punishment meted out to traitors—but he acceded to Ibn Ubayy's plea for clemency and spared them, provided that the whole tribe left Medina immediately. Qaynuqa' were ready to go. They had taken a gamble, but had underestimated Muhammad's new popularity. Neither their Arab allies nor the other Jews protested. Tribes had often been driven out of the oasis during the internecine wars before the hijrah, so this expulsion was part of a process that had started long before Muhammad's arrival.[28] Bloodshed was avoided, but Muhammad was caught in a tragic moral dilemma: the justification for the jihad against the Quraysh had been the Muslims' exclusion from their native city, which was condemned by the Qur'an as a great evil. Now, trapped in the aggressive conventions of Arabia, he was compelled to eject another people from their homeland.

The people of Medina anxiously waited for the inevitable Meccan attack. Since Abu Jahl had been killed at Badr and Abu Lahab had died shortly afterwards, Abu Sufyan was now the leading chieftain of the Quraysh and a far more formidable opponent. In the late summer, a contingent of Muslim ghazis captured a large Meccan caravan. Abu Jahl would have retaliated immediately, but Abu Sufyan did not allow this defeat to interfere with his long-term objectives. He simply intensified his preparations, building up a large confederacy of Bedouin allies. Once the winter rains were over, three thousand men with three thousand camels and two hundred horses left Mecca on March 11, 625 and began their journey northward. After a journey of a little over a week, they camped to the northwest of Medina on the plain in front of Mount Uhud.[29]

The Medinese had only a week's notice of the Meccan advance. There was no time to get the crops from the field, but Muhammad and the other chiefs managed to bring in the people from the outlying areas and barricade them into the "city." The experienced warriors urged caution. It was very difficult to sustain a siege in Arabia; and they suggested that everybody should stay behind the barricades and refuse to engage with the Quraysh, who would eventually be forced to retire. But after the victory at Badr, the younger generation wanted action and managed to carry the day. Muhammad, who was not the supreme commander, had to bow to this disastrous decision. The main Jewish tribes refused to fight and Ibn Ubayy withdrew his men from the army, so on the following morning, Muhammad faced the Quraysh outnumbered three to one. As the two armies began their advance, Abu Sufyan's wife Hind marched behind the Meccans with the other women, singing war songs and beating their tambourines. The Muslims were routed almost immediately with a brilliant charge by the Meccan cavalry. Muhammad was knocked senseless and word spread that he had been killed.

In fact, he had only been stunned, but the Quraysh did not bother to check the rumor and failed to follow up their advantage. The Muslim survivors were thus able to retreat in fairly good order.

Twenty-two Meccans and sixty-five Muslims had been killed, including Muhammad's uncle Hamzah, a renowned fighter. The Quraysh ran onto the battlefield and mutilated the corpses; one of them cut out Hamzah's liver and carried the gruesome trophy to Hind, who ate a morsel of it to avenge her brother, who had died by Hamzah's hand at Badr. She then cut off his nose, ears, and genitals, urging the other women to follow her example, and to the disgust of some of their Bedouin allies, they left the field sporting grisly bracelets, pendants, and collars. Before his army moved off, Abu Sufyan heard the disappointing news that Muhammad had not after all been among the casualties. "Next year at Badr!" he cried, as a parting challenge. "Yes!" one of the Muslims shouted on Muhammad's behalf, "It is an appointment between us!"[30]

The Muslim defeat could have been worse. Had the Quraysh followed up their charge, they could have destroyed the ummah. But the psychological impact of Uhud was catastrophic. When Muhammad returned home after the battle, sick and shaken, he heard loud lamentation outside the mosque: it was the wives of the Helpers mourning their dead. The Muslims fiercely resented Ibn Ubayy's refusal to fight. When he rose to speak in the mosque on the following Friday, one of the Helpers grabbed him and told him to keep his mouth shut. He strode from the mosque in fury and refused to ask for Muhammad's forgiveness. Hitherto the Hypocrites, as the Qur'an calls Ibn Ubayy's supporters, had been wavering, waiting to see how things would turn out; they now became openly hostile. Muhammad's victory at Badr, they claimed, had been a flash in the pan. He had brought death and destruction to Medina.

Each of the Muslim dead had left wives and daughters without protectors. After the defeat, a revelation came to Muhammad giving Muslims permission to take four wives. Muslims must remember that God had created men and women from a single living entity, so that both sexes were equally precious in his sight.

> Hence render unto the orphans their possessions and do not substitute bad things [of your own] for the good things [that belong to them] and do not consume their possessions together with your own; this, verily, is a great crime.

> And if you have reason to fear that you might not act equitably towards orphans, then marry from among [other] women such as are lawful to you—[even] two or three or four: but if you have reason to fear that you might not be able to treat them with equal fairness, then [only] one—or from among those whom you rightfully possess. This will make it more likely that you will not deviate from the right course.[31]

The institution of polygamy has been much criticized as the source of considerable suffering for Muslim women, but at the time of this revelation it constituted a social advance.[32] In the pre-Islamic period, both men and women were allowed several spouses. After marriage, a woman remained at the home of her family, and was visited by all her "husbands." It was, in effect, a form of licensed prostitution.

Paternity was, therefore, uncertain, so children were usually identified as the descendants of their mothers. Men did not need to provide for their wives and took no responsibility for their offspring. But Arabia was in transition. The new spirit of individualism in the peninsula meant that men were becoming more interested in their own children, were more assertive about personal property, and wanted their sons to inherit their wealth. The Qur'an encouraged this trend toward a more patriarchal society. Muhammad endorsed it by taking his wives into his own household and providing for them, and the verses instituting polygamy take it for granted that Muslim men will do the same. But the Qur'an was also aware of a social problem that this new revelation sought to redress.

In the pre-Islamic period, a woman could not own property. Any wealth that came her way belonged to her family and was administered by her male relatives. But in Mecca, where individualism was more pronounced than elsewhere in Arabia, some of the more aristocratic women had been able to inherit and administer their own fortunes. Khadijah was a case in point, but this was still rare in Mecca and almost unheard of in Medina. Most men found the idea that women could inherit and manage their property quite ludicrous. Women had no individual rights. How could they? Apart from a few notable exceptions, they did nothing to contribute to the economy; and because they took no part in the ghazu, they brought no wealth to the community. Traditionally women were considered part of a man's estate. After his death, his wives and daughters passed to his male heirs, who often kept them unmarried and impoverished in order to control their inheritance.

The Qur'anic institution of polygamy was a piece of social legislation. It was designed not to gratify the male sexual appetite, but to correct the injustices done to widows, orphans, and other female dependants, who were especially vulnerable. All too often, unscrupulous people seized everything and left the weaker members of the family with nothing.[33] They were often sexually abused by their male guardians or converted into a financial asset by being sold into slavery. Ibn Ubayy, for example, forced his women slaves into prostitution and pocketed the proceeds. The Qur'an bluntly refutes this behavior and takes it for granted that a woman has an inalienable right to her inheritance. Polygamy was designed to ensure that unprotected women would be decently married, and to abolish the old loose, irresponsible liaisons; men could have *only* four wives and must treat them equitably; it was an unjustifiably wicked act to devour their property.

The Qur'an was attempting to give women a legal status that most Western women would not enjoy until the nineteenth century. The emancipation of women was a project dear to the Prophet's heart, but it was resolutely opposed by many men in the ummah, including some of his closest companions. In a society of scarcity, it took courage and compassion to take financial responsibility for four women and their children. Muslims must have confidence that God would provide:

Marry the spouseless among you, and your
slaves and handmaidens that are righteous;
if they are poor, God will enrich them
of his bounty, God is all-embracing
   All knowing.[34]

Muhammad led the way. After Uhud, he took another wife, providing a home for Zaynab bint Khuzaymah, a widow whose husband had died at Badr. She was also the daughter of the Bedouin chief of 'Amir, and so the match forged a new political alliance. An apartment was built for her beside the mosque and she joined her "sisters"—Sawdah, 'A'isha and Hafsah—there.

The Prophet did not regard his women as chattel. They were his "companions"—just like the men. He usually took one of his wives along on a military expedition and disappointed his commanders by spending the whole of every evening in their tent, instead of bonding with his men. In the camp, the women did not remain meekly secluded, but walked around freely, taking an interest in everything that was going on. This type of freedom had been common for elite women in pre-Islamic Arabia, but it infuriated 'Umar. "Your boldness borders on insolence!" he yelled when he came one day upon 'A'isha strolling along the front lines. "What if disaster overtakes us? What if there is a defeat and people are taken captive?"[35] Muhammad's domestic arrangements gave his wives a new access to politics, and they seemed quite at home in this sphere. It would not be long before other women began to feel similarly empowered, and his enemies would use this women's movement to discredit the Prophet.

Muhammad had to recover the prestige he had lost at Uhud. He could not risk another open confrontation with the Quraysh, but nor could he afford to show his weakness. Two incidents in the summer of 625 showed how vulnerable he was. Two of the Bedouin tribes of Najd, a region to the west of Medina, had asked for instruction in Islam, so Muhammad sent six of his ablest men. During their journey they were attacked by one of the chiefs of Qudayd, the city of the goddess Manat, one of the three gharaniq. Three of the Muslims were killed; the others taken prisoner. One was stoned to death when he tried to escape and the other two were sold as slaves in Mecca, and afterwards taken outside the sanctuary and crucified.

At about the same time, Muhammad's new father-in-law, Abu Bara', chief of 'Amir, asked for help against warring factions in his own tribe. Forty Muslims were dispatched, and nearly all of them were massacred just outside 'Amir's territory, by members of the tribe of Sulaym. When one of the Muslim survivors came across two 'Amiris lying peacefully asleep under a tree, he killed them, assuming that their tribe had been responsible for the killing and taking revenge in the traditional fashion. When he returned to Medina, Muhammad told him that he had done wrong, but the tradition of retaliation was so deeply engrained in Arabia that it was nearly impossible to eradicate. Muhammad insisted on paying the usual compensation to Abu Bara'. His willingness to do so in spite of the fact that the crime had technically been committed by tribesmen of Sulaym made some of the Bedouin more kindly disposed towards the ummah. Some of the Sulaymites had been so impressed by the courage of their Muslim victims that they entered Islam themselves.

Muhammad's position in Medina remained precarious, and he could not afford to drop his guard. When he called upon the Jewish tribe of Nadir to collect the blood money for 'Amir, he narrowly escaped an assassination attempt: some members of Nadir had planned to drop a boulder on the Prophet from a nearby roof top. Ibn Ubayy had promised to support them and they probably assumed that Muhammad had been so discredited by Uhud that the Medinese would rally behind them. So they were astonished to receive a grim message from their former ally, the tribe of Aws: they had broken their treaty with the Prophet and could no longer remain in the city.

Like Qaynuqa' before them, the Nadiris withdrew to their fortress and waited for their allies to relieve them, but again no help was forthcoming. Even the powerful Jewish tribe of Qurayzah, which was also hostile to Muhammad, told them that they were on their own. After two weeks, Nadir knew that they could no longer sustain the siege, and when Muhammad gave the order to cut down their palm trees—an unmistakable sign of war in Arabia—they surrendered, begging only that their lives be spared. Muhammad agreed, on condition that they left the oasis immediately, taking with them only those goods that they could carry on their camels. So Nadir packed up their possessions, even taking down the lintels of their doors rather than leave them to Muhammad, and left Medina in a proud procession, as though they were going in triumph. The women dressed in all their jewels and finery, beating tambourines and singing to the accompaniment of pipes and drums. Weaving their way through the orchards and hamlets of the oasis, they finally took the road to Syria, though some stayed in the nearby Jewish settlement of Khaybar, where they helped Abu Sufyan build his confederacy against the Muslims by drumming up support among the northern tribes.[36]

In the space of two short years, Muhammad had expelled two powerful tribes from Medina, and the Muslims now managed the market vacated by Qaynuqa'. As we have seen, this was not Muhammad's intention. He had wanted to cut the cycle of violence and dispossession, not continue it. Muhammad had shown that he was still a man to be reckoned with, but he must also have reflected on the moral and political sterility of this type of success, because Nadir remained just as much of a threat in nearby Khaybar.

It was nearly time to make good on Abu Sufyan's parting shot after Uhud: "Next year at Badr!" but Muhammad was playing a very dangerous game. He had to make a show of strength, but his troops were so dispirited that he could not risk another pitched battle. Nevertheless, during the week of Badr's annual suq, he rode there with 1,500 men. Fortunately for the Prophet, Abu Sufyan did not appear. He had not expected the Muslims to keep the appointment and had set out with his army as a mere show, planning to turn back as soon as he heard that Muhammad had failed to leave Medina. It was a year of severe drought and there was not a blade of grass to feed the camels during the journey, so with only a few days' supplies packed, Abu Sufyan had to lead his men home. He was bitterly reproached by the Meccans, because the Bedouin were full of admiration for the Muslims' courage.[37]

In Medina, Muhammad's position was still weak.[38] But in the peninsula as a whole, the tide was beginning to turn in his favor. Whenever he heard that a Bedouin tribe had joined the Meccan confederacy, he would lead a ghazu to capture its flocks and herds—even if it meant a trek of five hundred miles to the Syrian border. In June 626, he learned that some clans of the Bedouin tribe of Ghatafan were planning a raid against Medina, so he set out to repel the expedition. When the Muslims came face to face with the enemy at Dhat al-Riqa, he once again avoided a direct confrontation, but for three days the Muslims remained face to face with the enemy. Both Tabari and Ibn Ishaq make it clear that the Muslim troops were terrified. But so, it seems, were the Ghatafan. In this atmosphere of terror, the Prophet received a revelation that instituted the Prayer of Fear, an abridged form of the usual prostrations adapted for a military emergency.[39] Instead of making themselves vulnerable to the enemy by praying en masse at the appointed times, Muslims should pray in relays, with their arms at the ready. In the end, the battle simply fizzled out before it began; Ghatafan withdrew and Muhammad could return to Medina, having achieved a symbolic victory.

The Prayer of Fear showed how beleaguered and defensive the new religion had become. It is in this context that we must see the Qur'an's apparent retreat from gender equality. In January 626, his new wife Zaynab had died, just eight months after their wedding. Not long afterwards, he approached Hind bint Abi Umayyah, the widow of his cousin Abu Salamah, who had died after Uhud, leaving her with four children. Hind—or Umm Salamah, as she was usually known—was twenty-nine years old; beautiful, sophisticated, and extremely intelligent, she would provide the Prophet with the kind of companionship he had enjoyed with Khadijah. She was also the sister of a leading member of Makhzum, one of the most powerful Meccan tribes. At first, she was reluctant to marry Muhammad. She had loved her husband very much, she explained; she was no longer young, had a jealous disposition, and was not sure that she could adapt to life in the harem. Muhammad smiled—he had a smile of great sweetness, which almost everybody found disarming—and assured her that in his late fifties, he was even older than she, and that God would cure her jealousy.

She was right to be wary, because life in the mosque was not easy.[40] The apartments of Muhammad's wives were so tiny that it was almost impossible to stand upright inside them. Muhammad did not have a house of his own. He passed the night with each of his wives in turn and her hut became his official residence for the day. There was practically no privacy, as Muhammad was constantly surrounded by crowds of people. He had frequent visits from his daughters and grandchildren. He was devoted to Hasan and Husayn, the sons of 'Ali and Fatimah, and was especially fond of his little granddaughter Umamah, whom he would carry into the mosque on his shoulders. He was constantly closeted with his closest companions: Abu Bakr,

Zayd, 'Ali, 'Uthman, and—increasingly—'Umar. As he became more widely respected in Arabia, he also received delegations from the Bedouin tribes, who crowded into the courtyard with their camels.

When he left the mosque after prayers, hordes of petitioners herded around their Prophet, pulling at his garments and yelling their questions and demands into his face.[41] They would follow him into his wife's hut, thronging round the table so tightly that it was sometimes impossible to pick up a morsel of food.[42] This was stressful for Muhammad, who was shy, fastidious, and sensitive to unpleasant bodily odors and bad breath. He was also getting older. He still had only a few grey hairs and walked so energetically that his feet seemed scarcely to touch the ground, but he was nearly sixty—a not inconsiderable age in Arabia, he had been injured at Uhud, and the constant pressure was beginning to tell on him at a time when the whole of Medina was waiting in terror for the inevitable return of the Meccan army and the ummah was more divided than ever before.[43]

This internal dissension became apparent as soon as Umm Salamah took up residence in the mosque. 'A'isha fiercely resented the arrival of this distinguished, superior woman, and a rift developed in the harem that reflected tensions within the ummah itself. Umm Salamah represented the more aristocratic Emigrants, while 'A'isha and Hafsah, the daughters of Abu Bakr and 'Umar, came from the more plebeian party in power. Each of Muhammad's wives sided with one of these two rival factions. Umm Salamah often relied upon the support of a third group, the *ahl al-beit*, the "people of the household," who were members of Muhammad's immediate family.

At the time of her marriage to Muhammad, these divisions were only in their infancy, but it would soon become clear that the ummah was not a monolithic group, and that the people who entered Islam had done so with very different expectations.

Umm Salamah quickly became the spokesperson for the women of Medina.[44] Muhammad's living arrangements, which had physically positioned his wives at the epicenter of the community, had given Muslim women a new vision of their role. 'A'isha and Hafsah were still young girls, and were sometimes flighty and selfish, but Umm Salamah was a very different proposition. Shortly after her marriage, a deputation of women asked her why they were mentioned so rarely in the Qur'an. Umm Salamah brought their question to the Prophet, who, as usual, took time to reflect upon it seriously. A few days later, while she was combing her hair in her apartment, she heard Muhammad reciting a revolutionary new surah in the mosque:

> Men and women who have surrendered,
> Believing men and believing women
> Obedient men and obedient women
> Truthful men and truthful women
> Enduring men and enduring women
> Men and women who give in charity
> Men who fast and women who fast,
> Men and women who guard their private parts
> Men and women who remember God oft—

> For them God has prepared forgiveness
> And a mighty wage.[45]

In other words, there was to be complete sexual equality in Islam; both men and women had the same duties and responsibilities. When the women heard these verses, they were determined to make this vision a concrete reality in their daily lives.

God seemed to be on their side. Shortly afterwards, a whole surah was dedicated to women. Women were no longer to be bequeathed to male heirs as though they were camels or date palms. They could themselves inherit and compete with men for a share in an estate.[46] No orphan girl should be married to her guardian against her will, as though she were simply moveable property.[47] As had been customary during the pre-Islamic period, women retained the power to initiate divorce proceedings, though the husband could refuse to comply. In Arabia, the groom traditionally presented a dowry to his bride, but in practice this gift had belonged to her family. Now the dowry was to be given directly to the woman as her inalienable property, and in the event of divorce, a man could not reclaim it, so her security was assured.[48] Qur'anic legislation insisted that the individual was free and sovereign—and that also applied to women.

In seventh century Arabia, this was a shocking innovation, and the men of the ummah were furious. God was taking away their privileges! They were ready to fight for him to the death, but now he was demanding sacrifice in their personal lives! The Medinese were particularly incensed; were they expected to divide their farms to give women a share? "How," they asked, "can one give the right of inheritance to women and children, who do not work and do not earn their living? Are they now going to inherit just like men who have worked to earn that money?" And was the Prophet seriously telling them that even an ugly girl could inherit a fortune? "Yes, absolutely," replied Muhammad.[49] Some tried to find a loophole in the legislation, but the women complained to Muhammad and the Qur'an supported them.[50]

The women made another demand: since raiding was so crucial to the economy, why could they not bear arms, too? Once again, Umm Salamah brought their question to the Prophet.[51] This went right to the heart of the ghazu economy. A woman who was taken prisoner during a raid was valuable booty; she could be sold, married, used for labor, or forced into prostitution. If women were allowed to fight instead of waiting passively to be taken prisoner, there would be a huge reduction of ghazu income. The controversy split the community and Muhammad was besieged by angry men who felt that Allah was emasculating them. 'Umar especially could not understand the Prophet's ridiculous leniency towards women. But Muhammad stood firm and insisted that God had made his will clear.

But the women had chosen the wrong moment to make their move. There was no way that the men would accept this at a time when the ummah faced extinction. The laws of inheritance and divorce remained in place, but Muhammad found that his enemies in Medina were making political capital out of this radical legislation and that he was opposed at this crucial juncture by some of his closest companions. Matters came to a head over the question of wife-beating.[52] The Qur'an forbade Muslims to inflict violence upon one another, and the women began to complain to the Prophet when their husbands hit them, demanding that they be punished as the Qur'an prescribed. Some even started to refuse sex to their abusive husbands. Muhammad was revolted by the very idea of violence towards women. "The Prophet never raised his hand against one of his wives, or against a slave, nor against any person at all," Ibn Sa'd recalled. He "was always against the beating of women."[53] But he was ahead of his time. Men like 'Umar, Ibn Ubayy, and even the gentle Abu Bakr beat their wives without giving the matter a second thought. Knowing that Abu Sufyan was mustering a massive army against Medina, Muhammad had to give way in order to retain the loyalty of his men. "Very well," he told his indignant companions, "beat them, but only the worst of you will have recourse to such methods."[54] A revelation seemed to give husbands permission to beat their wives but Muhammad did not like it.[55] "I cannot bear seeing a quick-tempered man beat his wife in a fit of anger," he said.[56] Yet again, the conflict with Mecca had compromised his vision and forced him to adopt a course of action that, in more normal circumstances, he would have preferred to avoid. The Qur'anic legislation about women is intertwined with verses about the war, which inevitably affected everything that happened in Medina at this time; Muhammad knew that he had no hope of surviving a Meccan onslaught with disaffected troops.

*

In March 627, a massive army of ten thousand men—the Quraysh and their confederates—were on the march toward Medina.[57] Muhammad could raise only a paltry three thousand warriors from Medina and his Bedouin allies. This time there was no stupid bravado; the Muslims barricaded themselves into the "city" in the center of the oasis. Surrounded on three sides by cliffs and plains of volcanic rock, Medina was not difficult to defend. It was most vulnerable from the north, but Muhammad adopted a stratagem suggested to him by Salman al-Farsi, a Persian convert. The Quraysh were in no hurry, making their way grandly and confidently in easy stages, so the Muslims had plenty of time. They gathered in the crops from the outlying fields, so that this time the Meccans would find no fodder, and then the entire community set to work digging a huge trench around the northern part of the oasis. This was nothing short of astonishing—even shocking—to Arab sensibilities. No self-respecting jahili warrior would dream of putting a barrier between himself and the enemy. He would consider it degrading to shovel earth like a slave. But Muhammad worked alongside his companions, laughing, joking, and singing with his men. Morale was high.

When the Quraysh arrived with their army, they stared blankly at the trench. The earth from the ditch had been used to build a high escarpment, which effectively shielded the Medinese in their camp and gave them a superior vantage point from which to hurl missiles. The Quraysh were bewildered. They had never seen anything so unsporting in their lives![58] Their cavalry, which was their pride and joy, was useless. From time to time, one of their horsemen would try to lead a dashing charge towards the enemy lines, only to screech absurdly to a halt when he arrived at the dugout.

The siege lasted only a month, but it seemed endless. Feeding and supplying the allies of Medina as well as their own people put a great strain on the city's resources. Ibn Ubayy and his party accused Muhammad of bringing ruin upon them[59] and the Jewish tribe of Qurayzah openly supported the Quraysh. The Jews of Khaybar had contributed a large squadron to the Meccan army, which included many of the exiled tribe of Nadir. Before the arrival of the Meccan army, Huyay ibn Akhtab, chief of Nadir, had tried to persuade Qurayzah either to attack the Muslims from the rear or to smuggle two thousand Nadiris into the oasis to slaughter the women and children in the fortresses. Initially Qurayzah were hesitant, but when they saw the vast Meccan army filling the plain in front of the city as far as the eye could see, their chief agreed to help the confederacy and provide the Quraysh with weapons and supplies. When Muhammad heard of this treachery, he was visibly distressed. He sent Sa'd ibn Mu'adh, who had been Qurayzah's chief Arab ally before the hijrah, to negotiate, but to no avail. At one point, the Qurayzah actually started to attack the fortresses on the southeast of the settlement, but the effort petered out. For about three weeks, it was quite unclear which way they would go.

Throughout the Battle of the Trench, as the siege became known, the Muslims were terrified. Faced with the prospect of extermination, some came close to despair. "Your eyes swerved and your hearts reached your throats," the Qur'an recalled, "while you thought strange thoughts about God; here it was that the believers were tried and shaken most mightily."[60] But even as those inside the city trembled, on the other side of the ditch, the Quraysh were becoming exhausted. They had inadequate provisions and their inexperience in military affairs meant that they were easily demoralized by a sudden reversal. Their resolve finally snapped when a violent rainstorm devastated their camp. Abu Sufyan recognized defeat. Horses and camels were dying, the Qurayzah had failed to deliver, and his troops had no tents, fires, or cooking pots. "Be off," he announced to his men, "for I am going."[61] When the Muslims peered over the escarpment the next morning, the plain was completely deserted.

But what was Muhammad to do about Qurayzah? The departure of the Quraysh had not weakened the bitter opposition to his leadership within Medina: His opponents were convinced that the Meccans would return in the not too distant future and wreak terrible vengeance for their humiliation, so they intensified their campaign against him. The settlement was on the brink of civil war and in this explosive climate, the Qurayzah could not remain unpunished. The day after the departure of the Meccan army, Muhammad's troops surrounded the fortress of Qurayzah, who asked that they be permitted to leave on the same terms as Qaynuqa' and Nadir. But this time Muhammad refused: Nadir had proved to be just as dangerous to the ummah in exile. The elders of Qurayzah agreed to accept the arbitration of their former ally Sa'd ibn Mu'adh, who had been severely wounded during the siege and was carried to the Qurayzah village on a litter. Even though some of the other tribes asked him to be merciful, Sa'd believed that the Qurayzah were an unacceptable security risk and made the conventional judgment: all seven hundred men of the tribe should be executed, their wives and children sold into slavery, and their property divided among the Muslims. When he heard the verdict, Muhammad is reported to have cried: "You have judged according to the ruling of Allah above the seven skies!"[62] The next day, the sentence was carried out.

Revolting as it seems to us today, almost everybody in Arabia would have expected Sa'd's judgment. According to the texts, not even the Qurayzah were surprised by the decision. The executions sent a grim message to the Jews of Khaybar, and the Bedouin would have noted that Muhammad did not shrink from retaliation. He had staged a defiant show of strength, which, it was hoped, would bring the conflict to an end. Change was coming to this desperate, primitive society, but for the time being, violence and killing on this scale were the norm.[63]

Nevertheless, the incident marks the nadir of Muhammad's career. It is, however, important to note that the Qurayzah were not killed on religious or racial grounds. None of the other Jewish tribes in the oasis either objected or attempted to intervene, clearly regarding it as a purely political and tribal matter. A significant number of the Arab tribe of Kilab, the clients of Qurayzah, were also executed alongside the Jews. Muhammad had no ideological quarrel with the Jewish people. He once said, "He who wrongs or destroys a Jew or a Christian will have me to answer on the Day of Judgment." The men of Qurayzah were executed for treason. The seventeen other Jewish tribes of Medina remained in the oasis, living on friendly terms with the Muslims for many years, and the Qur'an continued to insist that Muslims remember their spiritual kinship with the People of the Book:

> Do not argue with the followers of earlier revelation otherwise than in a most kindly manner—unless it be such of them as are bent upon evil-doing—and say: "We believe in that which has been bestowed from on high upon us, as well as that which has been bestowed upon you: for our God and your god is one and the same, and it is unto Him that We all surrender ourselves."[64]

Later in the Islamic empires, Jews would enjoy full religious liberty and anti-Semitism would not become a Muslim vice until the Arab/Israeli conflict became acute in the mid-twentieth century.

The tragedy of Qurayzah may have seemed expedient to the Arabs of Muhammad's time, but it is not acceptable to us today. Nor was it what Muhammad had set out to do. His original aim had been to end the violence of jahiliyyah, but he was now behaving like an ordinary Arab chieftain. He had felt impelled to go to war in order to achieve a final peace, but the fighting had unleashed a grim and vicious cycle of strike and counterstrike, atrocity, and retaliation, which violated essential principles of Islam. As he rode away from the village of Qurayzah towards a city that was still seething with resentment, Muhammad must have realized that he would have to find another way to end the conflict. Somehow he had to abandon this jahili behavior once and for all and find an entirely different solution.

Chapter Five

Salam

MUHAMMAD'S VICTORY over the Quraysh greatly enhanced his prestige in the peninsula. During the next few months, he capitalized on this, dispatching raiding parties against tribes who belonged to the Meccan confederacy, hoping to tighten the economic blockade that was damaging Qurayshan trade and attract some of the Syrian caravans to Medina. His continuing success made many of the Arabs question the validity of their traditional faith. They were pragmatic people, less interested in abstract speculation than in the effectiveness of a religious system. When the Meccan army had left Medina after the siege, the commander Khalid ibn al-Walid had cried: "Every man of sense now knows that Muhammad has not lied!"[1] Even the most committed adherents of the old faith were beginning to agree. During a raid against one of the Meccan caravans, Muhammad's former son-in-law Abu l-'As, who had been ready to give up his family rather than accept Islam, was taken prisoner; Muhammad ordered that he be released and his merchandise returned to him, and this second act of generosity so impressed Abu l-'As that after he had taken the goods back to Mecca, he made the hijrah, converted to Islam, and was reunited with Zaynab and their little daughter.

In Arabia as a whole, the tide had turned in Muhammad's favor, but within Medina the opposite was true. There the conflict had become more venomous than ever; every day Ibn Ubayy insinuated that had *he* retained the leadership, Yathrib could have been pacified without incurring the lethal enmity of the most powerful city in Arabia. Muhammad's enemies rarely attacked him openly, but conducted a somewhat underhanded smear campaign. His controversial attempt to improve the status of women was a godsend to them, and they began to circulate malicious and salacious rumors about his wives. Some made it known that they had their eye on some of the more attractive members of his harem and intended to marry them after his death—a suggestion that carried more than a hint of assassination.[2] It was whispered that Muhammad was now too old to satisfy his wives or that he had a testicular hernia.[3] There was a good deal of spiteful gossip about 'A'isha and a young man called Safwan ibn al-Mu'attal. When people crowded into his family quarters to put their questions and complaints to Muhammad, some of the men had actually insulted his wives before his very eyes. The situation was getting out of hand. At night, when it was cooler, Medina came to life, and people liked to walk about and socialize outside, enjoying the fresher air, but since the siege, women had been attacked on the streets. When the Prophet's wives went out together, the Hypocrites had started to follow them, yelling obscene sugges- tions and making lewd gestures.⁴ When challenged, they protested that in the darkness they had mistaken the women for slave girls, who were considered fair game for this type of harassment.

Muhammad was emotionally and physically drained by the strain of the last few years. He had always been emotionally dependent upon his women and this made him vulnerable. When he decided to take another wife, tongues started to wag again.⁵ Zaynab bint Jahsh had always been close to Muhammad; she was his cousin, but she was also the wife of Zayd, his adopted son. Muhammad had arranged the match himself shortly after the hijrah, even though Zaynab had been far from enthusiastic: Zayd was not physically pre- possessing and she may even then have been interested in Muham- mad himself. Zaynab was now in her late thirties, but, despite the harsh climate and conditions of Arabia, she was still extremely beau- tiful. A pious woman, she was a skilled leather-worker and gave all the proceeds of her craft to the poor. Muhammad seems to have seen her with new eyes and to have fallen in love quite suddenly when he had called at her house one afternoon to speak to Zayd, who happened to be out. Not expecting any visitors, Zaynab had come to the door in dishabille, more revealingly dressed than usual, and Muhammad had averted his eyes hastily, muttering "Praise be to Allah, who changes men's hearts!" Shortly afterwards, Zaynab and Zayd were divorced. The marriage had never been happy and Zayd was glad to release her. This story has shocked some of Muhammad's

Western critics who are used to more ascetic, Christian heroes, but the Muslim sources seem to find nothing untoward in this demonstration of their Prophet's virility. Nor are they disturbed that Muhammad had more than four wives: why should God not give his prophet a few privileges? What scandalized his opponents in Medina was the fact that Zaynab had been married to Zayd: Arabs regarded adoption as conferring an almost biological relationship and there was much scandalized talk about incest. Muhammad was reassured on this point by a revelation that assured him that Allah himself desired the match and that it was not sinful to marry the spouse of an adopted child.[6] 'A'isha, who was always prone to jealousy, happened to be with Muhammad when he received this divine message. How very convenient! she remarked tartly, "Truly thy Lord makes haste to do thy bidding!" As usual, tensions in the harem reflected divisions in the community as a whole: Muhammad's marriage to one of his own cousins would further the political ends of the Prophet's family, advancing the cause of the ahl al-beit.

Because of the scandal, Muhammad insisted that the entire community attend the wedding celebrations. The courtyard was crowded with guests, many of them hostile to the Prophet, and the atmosphere would not have been pleasant. Eventually the party began to break up, but a small group remained behind in Zaynab's new apartment, apparently blissfully unaware that it was time for the bride and groom to be alone. Muhammad left the room and sat with his other wives, hoping that these tactless guests would take the hint. "How do you like your new companion?" 'A'isha inquired acidly, when he dropped in on her. He eventually returned to Zaynab's hut, where the revellers were finally being ushered out by his friend Anas ibn Malik. As he entered the room, Muhammad somewhat impatiently drew a curtain (*hijab*) between himself and Anas, uttering the words of a new revelation:

> O you who have attained to faith! Do not enter the Prophet's dwellings unless you are given leave; [and when invited] to a meal, do not come [so early as] to wait for it to be readied: but whenever you are invited, enter [at the proper time]; and when you have partaken of the meal, disperse without lingering for the sake of mere talk: that, behold, might give offence to the Prophet, and yet he might feel shy of [asking] you [to leave]: but God is not shy of [teaching you] what is right.
>
> And as for the Prophet's wives, whenever you ask them for anything that you need, ask them from behind a screen: this will but deepen the purity of your hearts and theirs.[7]

The revelation went on to ordain that Muhammad's wives should not remarry after his death, and ordered them to wear their *jilbab* (which could refer to various garments) in a distinctive way, so that they could be recognized in the street and avoid harassment.[8]

The hijab verses have become extremely controversial.[9] They would eventually—about three generations after the Prophet's death—be used to justify the veiling of all women and their segregation in a separate part of the house. But they must be seen in context. They occur in Surah 33, which also deals with the siege, and must be considered against this frightening backdrop. These directives did not apply to all Muslim women, but only to Muhammad's wives. They were prompted by the thinly disguised threats of Muhammad's enemies, the aggressive encroachment upon his personal space, and the abuse to which his wives were subjected almost daily. The poisonous atmosphere of Medina after the siege had compelled Muhammad to change his personal arrangements. Henceforth there would be no open house; instead of crowding freely into his wives' apartments, Muslims must approach them from behind a protective screen. The word *hijab* comes from the root *HJB*: to hide. The curtain established a threshold; it shielded a "forbidden" or "sacred" (haram) object, like the damask cloth that covered the Kabah. In times of vulnerability, women's bodies often symbolize the endangered community, and in our own day, the hijab has acquired new importance in seeming to protect the ummah from the threat of the West.

Muhammad had not wanted to separate his private life from his public duties. He continued to take his wives on military expeditions, though they would now remain in their tent. But the other women of the ummah continued to move around the oasis freely. The hijab was not devised to divide the sexes. In fact, when the revelation had come down, the curtain had been drawn between two men—the Prophet and Anas—to separate the married couple from the hostile community. The introduction of the hijab was a victory for 'Umar, who had been urging the Prophet to segregate his wives for some time—a somewhat superficial solution to a complex problem. Muhammad had wanted to change people's attitudes, and the imposition of this external barrier was a compromise, because it did not require Muslims to exercise an internal control over their actions. But he gave in to 'Umar, because of the crisis that was tearing Medina apart.

But the situation did not improve. A few weeks after the introduction of the hijab, Muhammad's enemies orchestrated a vicious attack on 'A'isha, which devastated the Prophet and almost succeeded in dividing the community.[10] 'A'isha was an easy target. Everybody knew that she was Muhammad's favorite. She was beautiful, spirited, proud of her prominent position, jealous, outspoken, not without egotism, and had doubtless made many enemies. On this occasion, Muhammad had chosen 'A'isha to accompany him on an expedition against an ally of the Quraysh who had somewhat menacingly encamped a little closer to Medina than usual. According to Muhammad's spies, the Quraysh had persuaded them to attack the oasis. It was a successful raid: the Muslims intercepted them at the Well of Muraysi on the Red Sea coast and managed to carry off two hundred camels, five hundred sheep, and two hundred of their women. Juwayriyyah bint al-Harith, daughter of the chief, was among the captives. 'A'isha's heart sank as soon as she set eyes on her, because Juwayriyyah was so pretty, and, sure enough, during the negotiations that followed the raid,

Muhammad proposed marriage to seal the alliance with her father.

The Muslims camped at Muraysi for three days, but, despite the positive outcome of the ghazu, the simmering tension between the Emigrants and the Helpers escalated into a serious incident. While the Muslims were watering their camels at a well, local people from two different tribes—one confederated to the Quraysh, the other to the Khazraj—started to quarrel about a fairly trivial matter. Before long there was a full-scale brawl, and the combatants called upon the Muslim bystanders for help. The Emigrants rushed to the aid of the tribesmen who were allied to the Quraysh, while the Helpers from Khazraj rallied round their opponents. In a matter of moments, in direct violation of the Qur'an, Muslim was fighting Muslim. When they heard the news, 'Umar and some of Muhammad's other companions rushed in to stop this unseemly fighting, but Ibn Ubayy was enraged: how dared 'Umar prevent the Khazraj from helping their own allies! "They seek to take precedence over us!" he cried. "By Allah, when we return to Medina, the higher and mightier of us will drive out the lower and the weaker." A bystander ran immediately to report this to Muhammad, who paled when he heard this latest threat. 'Umar wanted to have Ibn Ubayy executed immediately, but Muhammad restrained him: did he want it said that the Prophet killed his own companions?" But he gave the Muslims orders to decamp immediately and begin the trek home, even though this meant travelling through the worst heat of the day—something he had never done before.

During one of the halts, 'A'isha slipped away to relieve herself, and when she returned, found that she had mislaid her necklace. It had been a wedding gift from her mother, and she could not bear to lose it, so she went back to search for it. While she was gone, the men lifted her litter—duly shrouded with the hijab—onto her camel, assuming that she was safely inside, and the party moved off without her. 'A'isha was not too distressed when she discovered the deserted campsite, because she knew that it was only a matter of time before somebody missed her. She sat down to wait and sure enough, her old friend Safwan ibn al-Mu'attal, who had fallen behind the others, turned up and put her on the back of his own camel. When 'A'isha rejoined the expedition with Safwan, the old rumor about their illicit relationship started up again, and Muhammad's enemies gleefully imagined the worst. It was not surprising that 'A'isha had fallen for Safwan, Ibn Ubayy remarked loudly, because he was so much younger and more attractive than her husband. The scandal rocked Medina, and the story seemed so plausible that some of the Emigrants began to believe it and even Abu Bakr, 'A'isha's father, began to suspect that it might be true.

More seriously, Muhammad himself began to doubt 'A'isha's innocence—a telling sign of his waning confidence during this difficult period. For a few days he seemed confused and uncertain. His need for 'A'isha was so great that, faced with the possibility of losing her, he seemed confused and hesitant. He no longer received any messages from God; it was the first time, since the very beginning of his prophetic career, that the divine voice had fallen silent. Ibn Ubayy continued to exploit the situation, and old tribal hatreds flared, as the Khazraj, Ibn Ubayy's tribe, threatened to fight the Aws, who argued that the people who were stirring the scandal should be immediately executed. The situation was so grave that Muhammad was forced to summon all the chiefs of Medina to a meeting and ask for their support should he find it necessary to take action against Ibn Ubayy, who was threatening his family.

Finally Muhammad went to confront 'A'isha, who had taken refuge in her parents' home. She had wept for two days but her tears dried like magic as soon as her husband entered the house and she faced him calmly. Muhammad urged her to confess her sin honestly; if she repented, God would forgive her. But with great dignity, the fourteen-year-old girl stood her ground and gazed steadfastly at her husband as she made her reply. There seemed little point in her saying anything at all, she said. She could not admit to something she had not done, and if she protested her innocence, nobody—not even her own parents—would believe her. She could only repeat the words of the prophet Jacob: "Patience in adversity is most goodly in the sight of God; and it is to God [alone] that I pray to give me strength to bear the misfortune which you have described to me."[12] She then turned silently and lay down on her bed.

Muhammad knew 'A'isha through and through, and she must have convinced him, because as soon as she had finished speaking, he fell into the deep trance that was so often a prelude to revelation. He swooned and Abu Bakr put a leather cushion under his head, while he and his wife waited, terrified, for God's judgment. "Good news, 'A'isha!" Muhammad cried at last: God had confirmed her innocence. Overcome with relief, her parents urged her to get up and come to her husband but 'A'isha remained implacable. "I shall neither come to him nor thank him," she replied. "Nor will I thank the both of you, who listened to the slander and did not deny it. I shall rise and give thanks to Allah alone!"[13] Duly chastened, Muhammad humbly accepted the rebuke, and went to recite the new revelation to the crowd that had gathered outside.[14] A personal and political tragedy had been averted, but doubts remained. The distressing incident had shown how vulnerable Muhammad was. Was he—as Ibn Ubayy had so cruelly suggested—a spent fire?

But in March 628, the month of the hajj pilgrimage to Mecca, Muhammad made a startling announcement that proved to be an extraordinary demonstration of his prophetic genius.[15] It seems that he had no clearly defined plan at the outset, but only a dimly perceived insight. He told the Muslims that he had had a strange, numinous dream: he had seen himself standing in the Haram of Mecca, with the shaven head of the pilgrim, wearing the traditional hajji costume and holding the key to the Kabah, filled with a serene assurance of victory. The next morning, he announced that he intended to make the hajj and invited his companions to accompany him. It is easy to imagine the fear, wonder, and uncertain joy that filled the Muslims when they heard this startling invitation. Muhammad made it clear that this would not be a military expedition. Pilgrims were forbidden to carry weapons during the hajj and he had no intention of violating the Meccan sanctuary where all fighting was forbidden. 'Umar objected. The Muslims would go like lambs to the slaughter! It was essential that they were able to defend themselves! But Muhammad was adamant. "I will not carry arms," he said firmly. "I am setting out with no other end than to make the pilgrimage." The pilgrims would wear no armour, but simply the traditional white robes of the hajji; at the beginning of the journey, they could carry a small hunting knife to kill game, but they would have to lay these aside once they had made their formal consecration. They would have to march unarmed into enemy territory.

None of the Bedouin who had joined Muhammad's confederacy was prepared to take the risk, but about a thousand Emigrants and Helpers volunteered. Even Ibn Ubayy and some of the Hypocrites decided to go; two women Helpers, who had been present at the Pledge of 'Aqabah, were allowed to join the party, and Umm Salamah accompanied Muhammad.

The Muslims set off with the camels that they would sacrifice at the climax of the hajj. At the first stop, Muhammad consecrated one of these camels in the traditional way, making special marks on it, hanging the ritual garments around its neck, and turning it in the direction of Mecca. He then uttered the pilgrim cry: "Here I am, O God, at your service!" The news of this audacious expedition spread quickly from one tribe to another, and the Bedouin followed their progress intently as the hajjis made the long journey south. Muhammad knew that he was placing the Quraysh in an extremely difficult position. Every Arab had the right to make the hajj and if the Quraysh, the guardians of the Haram, forbade a thousand pilgrims who were punctiliously observing the rites to enter the sanctuary, they would be guilty of a gross dereliction of duty. But it would also be intolerably humiliating for the Quraysh if Muhammad *did* enter the city, and it soon became clear that the Qurayshan leadership was determined to stop Muhammad at any price. In an emergency meeting of the Assembly, Khalid ibn al-Walid was dispatched with two hundred cavalry to attack the defenseless pilgrims.

When he heard this grave news, Muhammad was filled with anguish for his tribe. The Quraysh were so blinded by the sterile hatred of warfare that they were prepared to violate the sacred principles on which their entire way of life depended. What was the point of such intransigence? "Alas Quraysh!" he cried, "War has devoured them! What harm would they have suffered if they had left me and the rest of the Arabs to go our own ways?" The expedition was going to be quite different from what he had imagined. Because of his dream, Muhammad had probably expected to be admitted to Mecca, and have the opportunity to explain the principles of Islam to the Quraysh in the peaceful conditions imposed by the hajj. But he could not turn back now. "By Allah," he resolved, "I will not cease to strive for the mission with which God has entrusted me until he makes it victorious or I perish."[16] His first task was to get the pilgrims safely into the sanctuary. The Muslims found a guide from the friendly Bedouin tribe of Aslam, who led the party by a circuitous, rugged path into the area where all violence was forbidden. As soon as he entered the sacred zone, Muhammad reminded the pilgrims that they were engaged in a strictly religious activity. They must not allow themselves to be carried away by the excitement of homecoming; there must be no facile triumph; and they must put their sins behind them. Now they should make their way to the nearby well of Hudaybiyyah, getting their camels to kick up the sand so that Khalid and his men would know exactly where they were.

When they reached Hudaybiyyah, Muhammad's camel Qaswa' fell to her knees and refused to budge. The pilgrims yelled at her, trying to make her get up, but Muhammad reminded them of the elephant who had knelt before the Kabah during the Abyssinian invasion all those years ago—a divine "sign" that had persuaded the enemy army to turn back without a fight. Something similar was happening today. "The One who restrained the elephant from entering Mecca is keeping Qaswa' back," he explained, and yet again he reminded the pilgrims that they were coming in a spirit of reconciliation: "Whatever condition the Quraysh make in which they ask me to show kindness to kindred, I shall agree to."[17] Muhammad had never planned to overthrow the Quraysh but had simply wanted to reform the social system, which, he was convinced, would bring the city to ruin. The Quraysh thought that their pilgrimage amounted to a declaration of war but, like Qaswa', Muhammad was determined to prostrate himself humbly before the holiness of Mecca. The war had achieved nothing of lasting value and both sides had committed atrocities. This was to be a peaceful offensive, not an invasion.

But very few of the Muslims took Muhammad seriously. Keyed up by the excitement and drama of the occasion, they were expecting something spectacular. Perhaps there would be a miracle! Maybe they would enter Mecca in triumph and drive the Quraysh from the city! Instead, Muhammad calmly ordered them to water their camels and sit down beside them. What followed was what used to be called a "sit-in." Waiting obediently for permission to enter the city, refraining from violence, Muhammad was demonstrating that he was more in line with Arab tradition than the Quraysh, who had been prepared to kill him while he was making his way unarmed toward the sacred ground.

And, indeed, the Bedouin got the message. A chief of Khuza'ah who was visiting Mecca rode out to Hudaybiyyah to see what was going on. He was horrified to hear that the pilgrims had been denied access to the holy places, and went back to the city to protest angrily to the Quraysh. Mecca had always been an inclusive city; it had welcomed all Arabs to the Haram and this pluralism had been the source of its commercial success. What did they think they were doing? They had no right to bar a man who had clearly come in peace, he complained. But the Qurayshan elders laughed in his face. They were prepared to stand between Muhammad and the Kabah and fight him until their last man had been killed. "He may not have come wanting war," they cried, "but by Allah he shall never come in against our will, nor shall the Arabs ever say that we have allowed it."[18]

At this point, the Meccan resistance to Muhammad was led by Suhayl, the pious pagan whom Muhammad had hoped to attract to Islam, and the sons of some of Islam's earliest opponents: 'Ikrimah, who like his father, Abu Jahl, was implacably opposed to any compromise; and Safwan ibn Umayyah, whose father had died at Badr. Interestingly, Abu Sufyan seems to have played no part in the events of Hudaybiyyah. A man of outstanding intelligence, he probably realized that Muhammad had wrong-footed the Quraysh and that it was no longer possible to deal with him with the conventional defiance of jahiliyyah.

The Meccans had tried to kill the pilgrims, but Muhammad had eluded them; their next ploy was to try to cause dissension among the Muslims, by inviting Ibn Ubayy to perform the rites at the Kabah. But to everybody's surprise, Ibn Ubayy replied that he could not possibly perform the tawaf before the Prophet. He would clash with Muhammad again in the future, but at Hudaybiyyah, Ibn Ubayy was a loyal Muslim. Safwan and Suhayl persuaded 'Ikrimah to agree to negotiation, and sent one of their Bedouin allies, Hulays, chief of al-Harih, an extremely devout man, as their representative. When Muhammad saw him coming, he sent the sacrificial camels out to greet him, and when Hulays saw them trotting towards him, beautifully decked out in their garlands, he was so impressed that he did not even bother to interrogate Muhammad but returned immediately to the city. These were bona fide pilgrims, he reported, who must be admitted at once to the Haram. Safwan was furious. How dared Hulays—an ignorant Bedouin—give them orders! This was a grave mistake. Hulays rose and replied with great dignity:

You men of Quraysh, it was not for this that we made an alliance with you. Is a man who comes to do honor to the

house of Allah to be excluded from it? By Him who holds my
life in his hand, either you let Muhammad do what he has
come to do or I shall take away my troops to the last man.[19]

Safwan hastily apologized and asked Hulays to bear with them until
they found a solution that was satisfactory to everybody.

Their next envoy was 'Urwah ibn Mas'ud of Ta'if, a crucial ally
of Mecca. 'Urwah immediately put his finger on Muhammad's weak
spot. "So you have gathered this medley of people, O Muhammad,
by whom you came back to break the might of your own tribe," said
'Urwah, gesturing contemptuously at the pilgrims. "By Allah, I could
see these disbanding against you tomorrow!"[20] Muhammad knew
that despite this apparent show of strength and unity, he had very
few dependable allies. His Bedouin confederates, who had refused to
accompany him on the pilgrimage, had only a superficial commitment to Islam; his position in Medina was still desperately insecure;
and he knew that some of his closest companions would not understand what he was about to do. How could he realistically oppose the
Quraysh—his own tribe—with this motley rabble? The Quraysh, on
the other hand, were solidly united and armed to the teeth, 'Urwah
told him; even the women and children had vowed to prevent him
entering Mecca. Nevertheless, almost in spite of himself, 'Urwah was
impressed by the Muslims' devotion to the Prophet during this crisis,
and he told the Quraysh that—at least for the time being—Muhammad held the winning cards and they would have to make some kind
of agreement with him.

Muhammad decided to send an ambassador of his own into Mecca. First he dispatched one of the Helpers, thinking that this would be less inflammatory, but the Quraysh hamstrung the man's camel and would have killed him had not Hulays's tribesmen intervened. Next Muhammad approached 'Umar, but none of his clansmen in the city was strong enough to protect him, so it was decided that the well-connected 'Uthman ibn 'Affan should undertake the mission. The Quraysh heard him out, but were not convinced by his exposition of Islam, though they gave him permission to perform the rites of the pilgrimage. 'Uthman, of course, refused so the Quraysh decided to keep him as a hostage, but sent word to the Muslims that he had been killed.

This was a terrible moment. It seemed as though the expedition had horribly misfired. In this extremity, Muhammad fell into a trance but this time there was no message from Allah, and he had to find a solution himself, listening, as he always did, to the undercurrent of these fearful events in order to discover what was really going on. Finally, he asked the pilgrims to swear an oath of fealty. One by one, they took his hand and swore the Oath of Good Pleasure. The sources all have different interpretations of this event, but Waqidi's account is probably the most persuasive. He says that the Muslims vowed to obey Muhammad implicitly and to follow what was "in his soul" during this crisis.[21] Muhammad had never been able to command absolute obedience, but, shaken by the report of 'Uthman's murder, even Ibn Ubayy and the Hypocrites were ready to take the oath. Muhammad had resolved, at a deep instinctual level, to take a course of action that he knew many would find intolerable and he wanted to ensure their loyalty in advance. After everybody had taken the pledge, things began to improve. First came the good news that 'Uthman had not been killed after all, and then Muhammad saw Suhayl, whom he had always respected, approaching the camp, and realized that the Quraysh were now seriously prepared to negotiate.

This in itself was an important achievement. At last Muhammad had compelled the Quraysh to take him seriously, and there was a real possibility of a peaceful solution. Muhammad sat with Suhayl for a long time but the terms that were agreed filled many of his companions with dismay. First he promised to return to Medina without visiting the Haram, though Suhayl promised that the following year the Muslims could return and perform the traditional rites of the hajj within the city limits. There would be a truce between Mecca and Medina for ten years; Muhammad promised to return any member of the Quraysh who converted to Islam and made the hijrah to Medina without the consent of his guardians, but agreed that the Quraysh would not have to return a Muslim who defected to Mecca. The Bedouin tribes were released from their former treaty obligations and could choose to form an alliance with either Medina or Mecca.

The Qur'an had long stipulated that in the interests of peace, Muslims must agree to any conditions that the enemy proposed, even if they seemed disadvantageous.[22] But many of the pilgrims found these terms dishonorable. The truce meant that Muslims could no longer raid the Meccan caravans; why was Muhammad abandoning the economic blockade that was really starting to bite? Why had he consented to return new converts to Mecca, when the Quraysh did not have to reciprocate? During the last five years, many Muslims had died for their religion; others had risked everything and given up family and friends. Yet now Muhammad had calmly handed the advantage back to the Quraysh, and the pilgrims must agree to go home meekly, without even forcing the pilgrimage issue. The treaty assaulted every single jahili instinct. "The apostle's companions had gone out without any doubt of occupying Mecca, because of the vision the apostle had seen," explained Ibn Ishaq. "When they saw the negotiations for peace and a withdrawal going on and what the apostle had taken on himself, they felt depressed, almost to the point of death."[23]

Mutiny was in the air. The fragile solidarity that had united the pilgrims throughout this dangerous expedition was shattered and the deep rifts that had always existed within the ummah became suddenly apparent. 'Umar leapt to his feet and strode over to Abu Bakr. "Are we not Muslims and they polytheists?" he demanded. "Why should we agree to what is demeaning to our religion?"[24] Abu Bakr was also disturbed, but managed to reply that, in spite of everything, he still had faith in the Prophet. Later 'Umar said that if he could have found a hundred companions to follow him, he would have defected. At this point, he could not share Muhammad's vision.[25] Like many of the Medinese Muslims and those Emigrants who came from the more peripheral, disadvantaged Qurayshan clans, he did not want merely to reform the social order of Mecca but to overthrow it and replace it with a purely Qur'anic regime. 'Umar was courageous, unselfish, and passionately committed to the ideals of justice and equity, which had been so lacking in the Meccan polity. But he was not a man of hilm and was still fired by the fierce impetuosity of jahiliyyah. He did not understand that the values of gentleness and nonviolence were also central to the Islamic ideal. He was a man of action, prone to reach, jahili-like, for his sword without thinking matters through.[26] Faced with Muhammad's apparent about-face at Hudaybiyyah, he was bewildered and confused.

After defeating the Quraysh at the Battle of the Trench, the obvious plan would have been to press on and destroy them uni-laterally. But this had never been Muhammad's intention. The downfall of Mecca would be an inconceivable catastrophe for Arabia, a backward region that sorely needed the commercial genius of the Quraysh, who would never see the point of Islam while the war continued to fuel destructive anger and hatred on both sides. By abandoning the economic blockade, Muhammad hoped to win them over. He could see further than anybody else at Hudaybiyyah. Far from caving in weakly, he knew exactly what he was doing. He was moving toward an unprecedented political and religious solution for the Arabs, and that meant that he could never do the expected thing, because that would bind him to the unhappy status quo.

When he looked at the stunned, miserable faces of the pilgrims, Muhammad had to tell them that they must accept the terms of the treaty because Allah had dictated them. This did not satisfy the rank and file, who had expected some kind of miracle, and it was intensely disappointing to the Hypocrites, who had joined the ummah simply for worldly gain. The atmosphere became even more strained when the Muslims heard the wording of the treaty. Muhammad summoned ʿAli to write to his dictation, and when he began with the usual Muslim formula—"In the name of Allah, the Compassionate, the Merciful"—Suhayl objected. The Quraysh had always found these attributes of Allah somewhat feeble, so he insisted that Muhammad begin with the more conventional formula: "In thy name, O Allah." To the horror of the Muslims, Muhammad agreed without demur. Worse was to follow. Muhammad continued: "This is the treaty that Muhammad, the Messenger of Allah, has agreed with Suhayl ibn ʿAmr." Again Suhayl interrupted. If he had believed that Muhammad was God's prophet, he argued, reasonably enough, he would not have fought him all these years. He asked that Muhammad simply use his own name and that of his father in the usual way. ʿAli had already written down the words "the Messenger of God" and told Muhammad that he simply could not bring himself to excise them, so the Prophet held out his hand for the pen, asked ʿAli to point to the words on the parchment, and crossed them out himself. He continued: "This is what Muhammad ibn ʿAbdullah has agreed with Suhayl ibn ʿAmr."[27]

At this extremely difficult juncture, just as the treaty was being signed, Suhayl's son, Abu Jandal, burst onto the scene. He had converted to Islam, but Suhayl had locked him up in the family home in order to prevent him making the hijrah to Medina. Now, however, he had managed to escape and arrived triumphantly to join the Muslims at Hudaybiyyah, dragging his fetters behind him. Suhayl smashed his fist into his son's face, grabbed his chains, and turned to Muhammad. Would he keep his word and return this renegade to his lawful guardian? Muhammad did not falter, even though Abu Jandal screamed in anguish as Suhayl dragged him back to Mecca: "Am I to be returned to the polytheists that they may entice me from my religion, O Muslims?" With classic understatement, Ibn Ishaq remarks: "That increased the people's dejection."[28]

This was the last straw for 'Umar. Yet again, he jumped to his feet and yelled at the man he had followed so loyally for twelve years. Was he not God's messenger? Were not the Muslims right and their enemies wrong? Had not Muhammad assured them that they would pray again at the Kabah? This was all true, Muhammad replied mildly, but had he promised that they would return to the Haram this year? 'Umar remained grimly silent, so Muhammad continued firmly: "I *am* God's messenger. I will not go against his commandments and he will not make me the loser."[29] Even though he was bitterly perplexed, 'Umar subsided and reluctantly put his hand to the treaty. But the pilgrims were still furious and there was a dangerous moment when they seemed about to rebel. Muhammad announced that, even though they had not reached the Kabah, they would complete the pilgrimage right there at Hudaybiyyah: the Muslims must shave their heads and sacrifice their camels, just as they would if they were in the heart of Mecca. There was absolute silence, and the pilgrims stared grimly back at Muhammad, tacitly refusing to obey. In despair, the Prophet retreated to his tent. What on earth could he do? he asked Umm Salamah. She judged the situation perfectly. Muhammad should go out and, without uttering another word, sacrifice the camel that he had consecrated to Allah. It was exactly the right decision. The spectacular bloodletting broke through the torpor of depression, and immediately the men fell over themselves to sacrifice their own camels and shaved each other's heads with such zeal that Umm Salamah said later that she thought they would inflict mortal wounds in their pious frenzy.

The pilgrims started home in a lighter mood, but some anger remained and the Prophet himself seemed distant and preoccupied. 'Umar was afraid that his defiance had irreparably damaged their friendship, and his heart sank when he was summoned to join Muhammad at the head of the party. But to his intense relief, he found him looking radiant, as though a great weight had fallen from his shoulders. "A surah has descended upon me, which is dearer to me than anything under the sun," he told 'Umar.[30] This was *Al-Fatah*, the Surah of Victory. It laid bare the deeper meaning of the events of Hudaybiyyah and began with a luminous assurance that Muhammad had not suffered a diplomatic defeat there but that God had given him "a manifest victory." He had sent down his *sakinah*, the spirit of peace and tranquillity, which had entered the hearts of the Muslims; they had made a courageous act of faith when they had agreed to accompany Muhammad on this perilous expedition—showing a commitment that had been beyond the

Bedouin. They had shown their faith and trust again when they had sworn the Oath of Good Pleasure. Finally, the treaty that Muhammad had made with Mecca was a "sign," an ayah, which revealed God's presence.

The victory at Hudaybiyyah had distinguished the Muslims from the Quraysh, who had shown throughout the day that they were still in thrall to the overbearing haughtiness and intransigence of the jahiliyyah, a stubborn resistance to anything that might injure their sense of honor or their traditional way of life. They had even been ready to massacre the innocent unarmed pilgrims rather than accept the "humiliation" of admitting them to the Haram.

> When in the hearts of those who persist in unbelief arose the characteristic arrogance, the arrogance of jahiliyyah, then God sent down his peace of soul (sakinah) upon His Messenger and upon the believers, and imposed upon them the formula of self-restraint (hilm), for that was most befitting to them and they were most suited for that.[31]

Muslims were not supposed to be men of war; they were characterized by the spirit of hilm, a peace and forbearance that allied them with the Jews and Christians, the People of the Book. Instead of posturing aggressively as the Quraysh had done at Hudaybiyyah, the true followers of Allah prostrated themselves humbly before God in prayer:

Thou seest them bowing, prostrating, seeking bounty from
God and good pleasure. Their mark is on their faces, the trace
of prostration. That is their likeness in the Torah, and their
likeness in the Gospel.

It was not violence and self-assertion, but the spirit of mercy,
courtesy and tranquillity that would cause the ummah to grow, "as a
seed that puts forth its shoot and strengthens it and it grows stout
and raises straight upon its stalk, pleasing the owners."[32] The war was
over; it was now time for a holy peace.

In fact the struggle would continue, but the sources agree that
Hudaybiyyah was a watershed. "No previous victory (fatah) was
greater than this," Ibn Ishaq believed. The root meaning of *FTH*
was "opening;" the truce had looked unpromising at first, but it
opened new doors for Islam. Hitherto nobody had been able to sit
down and discuss the new religion in a rational manner, because of
the constant fighting and escalating hatred. But now "when there
was an armistice and men met in safety and consulted together,
none talked about Islam intelligently without entering it." Indeed,
between 628 and 630, "double as many or more than double as many
entered Islam as ever before."[33] The short lyrical surah *An-Nasr*
("Help") may have been composed at this time:

When the help of God arrived
    and the opening (fatah)
and you saw people joining the religion of God in waves

Recite the praise of your Lord
  and say God forgive
He is the always forgiving.[34]

There was to be no triumphalism, no cry for vengeance. The new era must be characterized by gratitude, forgiveness, and an acknowledgement of the Muslims' own culpability.

Hudaybiyyah may have improved the position of Islam in the peninsula as a whole, but, like other recent advances, it did little for Muhammad's standing in Medina. Many of the pilgrims— Helpers and Emigrants alike—continued to feel cheated and resentful. How, the Emigrants asked, were they supposed to earn a living if they could no longer attack the Meccan caravans? Muhammad knew that he could not allow this discontent to fester; somehow he had to find a way of compensating them without damaging the truce, so after Hudaybiyyah, he directed the Muslims' attention to the north, away from Mecca. Khaybar—the new home of the exiled Jewish tribe of Nadir—was still a danger. The leaders of the settlement continued to stir up hostility to Muhammad among the northern tribes, so shortly after his return from Hudaybiyyah, he set off to besiege the city with an army of six hundred men. When the Quraysh heard the news, they were jubilant, certain that the Muslims would be defeated. Surrounded, like Medina, with plains of volcanic rock and defended by seven large fortresses, Khaybar was thought to be impregnable. But the Muslims were able to benefit from the internal strife that signalled the decline of the tribal spirit in Khaybar, as it had in Medina. Each of the tribes of Khaybar was autonomous, and they found it impossible to cooperate effectively during the siege. To add to their troubles, the tribes of Ghatafan, whose support they had been expecting, failed to show up, so after a month the Jewish elders asked for peace and became vassals of Medina. To seal the agreement, Muhammad took the daughter of his old enemy Huyay, chief of Nadir, as his wife. The beautiful seventeen-year-old Safiyyah was happy to enter Islam, and Muhammad gave stern orders that there were to be no unkind remarks about her father, who had died during the siege. He told Safiyyah that if any of his other wives taunted her about her Jewish ancestry, she should reply: "My father is Aaron and my uncle is Moses."[35] The marriage expressed the attitude of reconciliation and forgiveness that he was trying to promote; it was time to lay aside the hatred and bloodshed of the past.

On his return from Khaybar, Muhammad enjoyed a joyful family reunion. After Hudaybiyyah, he had sent a message to the Muslim exiles still resident in Abyssinia, inviting them to return now that the situation in Arabia had improved, and when he returned home, his cousin Ja'far, Abu Talib's son, whom he had not seen for thirteen years, was waiting for him in Medina. He also greeted yet another new wife. Earlier that year, he had learned that his cousin 'Ubaydallah ibn Jahsh had died in Abyssinia, and decided to marry his wife Ramlah, usually known by her kunya, Umm Habibah. The ceremony was performed by proxy before the Negus, and an apartment had already been prepared for her in the mosque. This was another shrewd political move, because Umm Habibah was the daughter of Abu Sufyan.

The rest of the year was spent in routine raiding, some of which was undertaken at the request of his new Jewish allies in the north. Then in March 629, the month of the hajj, it was time for Muhammad to lead another pilgrimage to the Kabah. This time 2,600 pilgrims accompanied him, and as they approached the sanctuary, the Quraysh evacuated the city, as they had agreed. The Qurayshan elders watched the arrival of Muhammad from the top of a nearby mountain. The sound of the Muslims loudly announcing their presence with the traditional cry: "Here I am, O Allah! Here I am!" must have echoed through the valleys and empty streets of the city like a cruel taunt. But they must also have been impressed by the discipline of the Muslims. There were no scenes of unbridled joy or unseemly celebrations; no jeering at the Quraysh. Instead, the huge crowd of pilgrims filed slowly and solemnly into the city, led by Muhammad, who as usual was mounted on Qaswa'. When he reached the Kabah, he dismounted and kissed the Black Stone, embracing it, and then proceeded to make the circumambulations, followed by the entire pilgrim body. It was a strange homecoming. The Emigrants must have felt highly emotional about their return, and yet, although the city was a ghost town, they were not free to do as they pleased. It had been settled at Hudaybiyyah that this year the Muslims could only make the Lesser Pilgrimage, the umrah, which did not include a visit to Mount 'Arafat and the valley of Mina.

In temporary exile from their city, the Quraysh had to watch—no doubt appalled—as Bilal, a former slave, climbed onto the roof of the Kabah and summoned the Muslims to prayer. Three times a day, his huge voice reverberated through the valley, urging all within earshot to come to salat with the cry "Allahu Akhbar," reminding them that Allah was "greater" than all the idols in the Haram, who could do nothing to prevent this ritual humiliation. It was an immense triumph for Muhammad, and many of the younger Quraysh became even more convinced that the old religion was doomed.

On his last evening in the city, Muhammad enjoyed another family reunion when his uncle 'Abbas, who still adhered to the old religion, was allowed to enter the city to visit his nephew and offer him the hand of his sister Maymunah, who had been recently widowed. Muhammad accepted, doubtless hoping to entice 'Abbas himself into Islam, and mischievously sent word to the Quraysh to invite them to the wedding. This was pushing things too far, and Suhayl came down to inform Muhammad that his three days were up and he should leave immediately. Sa'd ibn 'Ubadah, a chief of Khazraj who was with the Prophet at the time, was furious at this apparent discourtesy, but Muhammad quickly silenced him: "O Sa'd, no ill words to those who have come to visit us in our camp."[36] To the astonishment of the Quraysh, the entire pilgrim throng left the city that night in good order. There were no loud protests, no attempt to repossess their old homes. In their peaceful withdrawal, the Muslims showed the confidence of those who expected a speedy return.

The story of this strange pilgrimage spread rapidly, and more and more of the Bedouin came to Medina to become Muhammad's confederates. Of even greater significance was the steady stream of the younger generation of the Quraysh who converted to Islam. At Hudaybiyyah, Muhammad had promised to return new converts to Mecca, but he had been able to find a loophole that enabled him to overcome this condition on a technicality. First, the treaty had said nothing about the handing back of women converts, so shortly after Hudaybiyyah, Muhammad had received 'Uthman's half-sister into the ummah and allowed her to remain. He did, however, return Abu Basir, an impetuous young man, and dispatched him to Mecca with a Qurayshan envoy. But during the journey, Abu Basir killed his escort, and when Muhammad sent him away again, set up camp on the Red Sea coast near the trade route, where he was joined by seventy other young Meccan malcontents. These would-be Muslims became highwaymen, attacking every single Meccan caravan that came within their range, and the Quraysh discovered that the economic blockade had been partially reinstated. Eventually they were forced to beg Muhammad to admit the young men into Medina and to make them abide by the treaty.

So the ban on accepting converts became a dead letter, and in 629 a steady stream of new Muslims arrived in Medina. They included the young warriors 'Amr ibn al-'As and Khalid ibn al-Walid, who had been convinced by Muhammad's success. "The way has become clear," Khalid said, "the man is certainly a prophet."[37] He was afraid of reprisals, since he and 'Amr had both killed many Muslims at the battles of Uhud and the Trench, but Muhammad assured them that the act of islam wiped out old debts and represented an entirely new start.

In this year of political triumph, Muhammad had a private joy. None of the women he had married in Medina had borne him any children, but the governor of Alexandria in Egypt had sent him a beautiful, curly-haired slave girl as a gift. Maryam was a Christian and did not wish to convert to Islam, but she became Muhammad's *saraya*, a wife who retained the status of a slave but whose children would be free. Muhammad grew very fond of her, and was overjoyed when at the end of 629 she became pregnant. He named their son Ibrahim, and loved carrying him around Medina, inviting all passers-by to praise the baby's beautiful complexion and his likeness to himself. However, sorrow came along with joy. Muhammad's daughter Zaynab had died shortly after he made the Lesser Pilgrimage, and later that year he lost two members of his family in a disastrous expedition to the Syrian border. We know very little about this ill-fated campaign. Muhammad may have wanted to bring the Christian Arab tribes there into the ummah as confederates, on the same basis as the Jewish tribes of Khaybar. At all events, he dispatched Zayd and his cousin Ja'far to the north at the head of an army of three thousand men. At the village of Mu'tah near the Dead Sea the Muslims were attacked by a detachment of Byzantines. Zayd, Ja'far, and ten other Muslims were killed and Khalid, who had also accompanied the expedition, decided to bring the troops home.

When Muhammad heard the news, he went directly to Ja'far's

house, distraught to think that he had brought his dear cousin home to his death. Asma', Ja'far's wife, was baking bread, and as soon as she saw the expression on Muhammad's face, she knew that something terrible had happened. Muhammad asked to see their two sons, knelt down beside the little boys, hugged them close and wept. Immediately Asma' began to lament in the traditional Arab way, the women hurried to her, and Muhammad asked them to make sure to bring the family food during the next few days. As he walked through the streets to the mosque, Zayd's little girl ran out of their house and threw herself into his arms. Muhammad picked her up and stood there in the street, rocking her and weeping convulsively.

The defeat at Mu'tah had further jeopardized Muhammad's position in Medina. When Khalid brought the army home, he and his men were booed and hissed, and Muhammad had to take Khalid under his personal protection. But in November 629, the situation in Arabia changed dramatically: the Quraysh broke the treaty of Hudaybiyyah. Aided and abetted by some of the Quraysh, the tribe of Bakr, one of their Bedouin allies, made a surprise attack on the tribe of Khuza'ah, which had joined Muhammad's confederacy. Khuza'ah promptly asked Muhammad for help and the Quraysh woke up to the fact that they had given Muhammad a perfect excuse to attack Mecca. Safwan and 'Ikrimah remained defiant, but Suhayl was beginning to have second thoughts. Abu Sufyan, however, went further and arrived in Medina on a peace initiative.

At this point, Abu Sufyan had no desire to convert to Islam, but he had realized for some time that the tide had turned in favor of

Muhammad and that the Quraysh must try to get the best deal they could. In Medina he visited his daughter Umm Habibah, and sat in conference with some of Muhammad's closest companions, trying to find a way of distancing himself from the dispute. Then he returned to Mecca, where he tried to prepare his fellow-tribesmen to accept the inevitable. After his departure, Muhammad began to plan a new campaign.

On 10 Ramadan (January 630), Muhammad set out at the head of the largest force ever to leave Medina. Nearly all the men in the ummah had volunteered and along the road their Bedouin allies joined forces with the Muslims, bringing the numbers up to ten thousand men. For security reasons, the destination of the expedition remained secret, but there was naturally a good deal of excited speculation. Certainly Mecca was a possibility, but Muhammad could just as easily have been heading for Ta'if, which was still implacably hostile to Islam, so the southern tribe of Hawazin started to assemble a massive army there. In Mecca, the Qurayshan leaders feared the worst. 'Abbas, Abu Sufyan, and Budayl, chief of Khuza'ah, all made their way under cover of night to the Muslim camp. There Muhammad received them and asked Abu Sufyan if he was ready to accept Islam. Abu Sufyan replied that even though he now believed that Allah was the only God—the idols had proved to be useless—he still had doubts about Muhammad's prophethood. But he was shocked and impressed when he watched all the members of the massive army prostrating themselves in the direction of Mecca during the morning prayer, and when he saw the various tribes marching past on their way to the city, he knew that the Quraysh must surrender.

He hurried back to Mecca and summoned the people by crying at the top of his voice: "O Quraysh, this is Muhammad who has come to you with a force you cannot resist!" He then offered them an option that had been suggested to him by 'Ali during his visit to Medina. Anybody who wanted to surrender should put himself under his personal protection: Muhammad had agreed to honor this. They should either take sanctuary in his home or remain in their own houses. Hind, his wife, was beside herself with rage; seizing him by his moustaches, she yelled to the townspeople: "Kill this fat greasy bladder of lard! What a rotten protector of his people!" But Abu Sufyan begged them not to listen. He described what he had seen in the Muslim camp. The time for such defiance was over. His grim sobriety impressed most of the Quraysh. Pragmatic to the last, they barricaded themselves into their houses as a token of surrender.

A few wanted to fight, however. 'Ikrimah, Safwan, and Suhayl gathered a small force and tried to attack Khalid's section of the army as it approached the city, but they were quickly beaten. Safwan and 'Ikrimah fled, thinking their lives were at stake; Suhayl laid down his arms, and retired to his home. The rest of the Muslim army entered Mecca without striking a single blow. Muhammad had his red tent pitched near the Kabah and there he joined Umm Salamah and Maymunah, the two Qurayshi wives who had accompanied him, together with 'Ali and Fatima. Shortly after they had settled, 'Ali's sister Umm Hani' arrived to plead for the lives of two of her relatives who had taken part in the fighting. Even though 'Ali and Fatima wanted them executed, Muhammad immediately promised that they would be safe. He had no desire for bloody reprisals. Nobody was made to accept Islam nor do they seem to have felt any pressure to do so. Reconciliation was still Muhammad's objective.

After he had slept for a while, he rose, and performed the morning prayer. Then, mounted on Qaswa', he rode round the Kabah seven times, crying "Allahu Akhbar!" The shout was taken up by the troops and soon the words rang through the entire city, signalling the final victory of Islam. Next Muhammad turned his attention to the idols of the Haram; crowded onto their roofs and balconies, the Quraysh watched him smash each stone effigy while he recited the verse: "The truth has come, and falsehood has vanished away; surely falsehood is certain to vanish."[38] Inside the Kabah, the walls had been decorated with pictures of the pagan deities, and Muhammad ordered them all to be obliterated, though, it is said, he allowed frescoes of Jesus and Mary to remain.

By this time, some of the Quraysh had ventured forth from their houses and made their way to the Kabah, waiting for Muhammad to leave the shrine. He stood in front of the house of Allah and begged them to lay aside the arrogance and self-sufficiency of jahiliyyah, which had created only conflict and injustice. "O Quraysh," he cried, "Behold God has removed from you the arrogance of jahiliyyah with its boast of ancestral glories. Man is simply a God-conscious believer or an unfortunate sinner. All people are children of Adam, and Adam was created out of dust."[39] Finally Muhammad quoted the words that God had spoken to the whole of humanity:

Behold, we have created you all out of a male or a female, and
have made you into nations and tribes, so that you may come
to know one another. Verily, the noblest of you in the sight
of God is the one who is most deeply conscious of him.
Behold God is all-knowing, all-aware.[40]

The true karim was no longer an aggressive chauvinist, but was filled
with reverent fear. The purpose of the tribe and the nation was
no longer to exalt its superiority; they must not seek to dominate,
exploit, convert, conquer, or destroy other peoples, but get to
know them. The experience of living in a group, coexisting with
people—some of whom, despite their kinship, would inevitably be
uncongenial—should prepare the tribesman or the patriot for the encounter with foreigners. It should lead to an appreciation of the
unity of the human race. Muhammad had managed to redefine the
concept of nobility in Arabia, replacing it with a more universal,
compassionate, and self-effacing ideal.

But were the Quraysh ready for this? Muhammad issued a gen-
eral amnesty. Only about ten people were put on the Black List; they
included 'Ikrimah (but not Safwan, for some reason), and those who
had spread anti-Muslim propaganda or injured the Prophet's family.
Some of these miscreants asked for pardon, however, and they seem
to have been spared. After his speech beside the Kabah, Muhammad
withdrew to Mount Safa and invited the people of Mecca to swear
fealty. One by one, the Quraysh filed up to Muhammad, who sat
flanked by 'Umar and Abu Bakr. One of the women who came

before him was Hind, Abu Sufyan's wife, who was on the Black List for her mutilation of Hamzah's body after the battle of Uhud. She remained defiant. "Forgive me what is past," she said, with no hint of apology, "and God will forgive you!" Muhammad asked her if she would undertake not to commit adultery, theft, or infanticide. Would she promise not to kill her children? To this Hind replied: "I brought them up when they were little, but you killed them on the day of Badr when they were grown up." Muhammad tacitly conceded the point.⁴¹ Hind decided to convert to Islam, telling Muhammad that he could not continue to proceed against her now that she was a professing Muslim. The Prophet smiled and told her that of course she was free. Soon, Hind would see her husband and sons given important office in the ummah as a reward for Abu Sufyan's cooperation.

Relatives of Safwan and 'Ikrimah begged for their lives; Muhammad promised that, if they accepted his leadership, they were free to enter Mecca. Both decided to return and 'Ikrimah was the first to accept Islam. Muhammad greeted him affectionately and forbade anybody to vilify his father, Abu Jahl. Safwan and Suhayl both swore fealty to Muhammad but could not yet make the Muslim profession of faith—though they changed their minds a few days later.

Once Muhammad had secured the city, he had to deal with the tribes of Hawazin and Thaqif, who had mustered an army of twenty thousand men at nearby Ta'if. Muhammad managed to defeat them at the battle of Hunayn at the end of January 630 and the Hawazin joined Muhammad's confederacy. The Muslims were not able to take Ta'if itself, but the city became so isolated through the loss of its chief Bedouin ally that it was forced to capitulate a year later. When he divided the booty after his victory at Hunayn, Muhammad gave Abu Sufyan, Suhayl, and Safwan the lion's share. Safwan was so overcome that he instantly made his surrender. "I bear witness that no soul could have such goodness as this, if it were not the soul of the Prophet," he cried. "I bear witness that there is no god but Allah and that you are his Messenger."[42] Suhayl followed his example.

Some of the Helpers were offended by this apparent favoritism. Did it mean that Muhammad would abandon them, now that he had been reunited with his own tribe? Muhammad instantly reassured them by making a moving speech, which reduced many of them to tears. He would never forget their generosity to him while he was a mere refugee, and promised that—far from settling in Mecca—he would make Medina his home for the rest of his life. "Are you not satisfied that other men should take away flocks and herds while you take back with you the apostle of God?" he asked. "If all men went one way and the Helpers another, I should take the way of the Helpers. God have mercy on the Helpers, their sons and their sons' sons."[43]

It was a strange conquest, and an impartial observer might have wondered why the Muslims and the Quraysh had fought at all.[44] Muhammad kept his word and returned to Medina with the Emigrants and Helpers. He did not attempt to rule Mecca himself; nor did he replace the Qurayshan officials with his own companions; nor did he establish a purist Islamic regime. All former dignitaries kept their positions in the Haram, and the assembly and the status quo remained intact. His most hated enemies were not only reinstated but promoted and showered with gifts. When Muhammad was about to reassign the most prestigious function of the Haram—that of providing water to the pilgrims—to the notable who had just given him the keys of the Kabah, Muhammad asked him: "You can surely see now that this key is in my hand, that I can assign it to whomever I want?" The notable, thinking that the office would now go to one of the Muslims, cried in anguish: "Then, the glory and might of Quraysh is gone!" Muhammad promptly replied, as he handed back the key: "To the contrary, today it is entrenched and glorious!"[45]

Muhammad's work was almost done. After his return home, the opposition in Ibn Ubayy's camp continued. There was yet another plot to assassinate Muhammad, who tried to woo his enemies by dispatching more lucrative expeditions to the north. In October 631, he became aware that a mosque in Medina had become a center of disaffection, so he was forced to destroy it. The following morning he held an inquiry into the conduct of the people who had been plotting against him; they hastily apologized. Most offered plausible excuses and were pardoned, though three were formally shunned by the ummah for nearly two months. This seems to have finished the Muslim opposition. Not long after this capitulation, Ibn Ubayy died, and Muhammad stood beside the grave of his old adversary as a mark of respect. He had finally managed to create a viable, united society in Medina, and more and more of the Bedouin were prepared to accept his political supremacy, even though they were not committed to his religious vision. In ten short years since the hijrah, Muhammad had irrevocably changed the political and spiritual landscape of Arabia.

However, he was visibly failing, and by the beginning of 632, increasingly conscious that he was approaching the end of his life. He was immensely distressed when his baby son Ibrahim died, and he wept bitterly, though he was certain that he would soon be with him in Paradise. But when the traditional month for the hajj approached, he announced that he would lead the pilgrimage and set out at the end of February with all his wives and a huge crowd of hajjis, arriving outside Mecca in early March. He led the Muslims through the rituals that were so dear to the hearts of the Arabs, giving them a new significance. Instead of being reunited with their tribal deities, the Muslims were to gather round the "house"—the Kabah—built by their ancestors Abraham and Ishmael. When they ran seven times between Safa and Marwah, Muhammad instructed the pilgrims to remember the distress of Hagar, Ishmael's mother, when, after Abraham had abandoned them in the wilderness, she had run frantically to and fro in search of water for her baby. God had saved them by causing the spring of Zamzam to well up from the depths of the earth. Next the pilgrims recalled their unity with the rest of humanity, when they made a standing vigil on the slopes of Mount 'Arafat, where, it was said, God had made a covenant with Adam, the father of the entire human race. At Mina, they threw stones at the three pillars as a reminder of the constant struggle (jihad) with temptation that a godly life required. Finally, they sacrificed a sheep, in memory of the sheep Abraham sacrificed after he had offered his own son to God.

Today the mosque of Namira stands near Mount 'Arafat on the spot where Muhammad preached his farewell sermon to the Muslim community. He reminded them to deal justly with one another, to treat women kindly, and to abandon the blood feuds and vendettas inspired by the spirit of jahiliyyah. Muslim must never fight against Muslim. "Know that every Muslim is a Muslim's brother, and that the Muslims are brethren. It is only lawful to take from a brother what he gives you willingly, so wrong not yourselves," Muhammad concluded, "O God, have I not told you?" There was pathos in this last appeal. Muhammad knew that despite his repeated admonitions, not all Muslims fully understood his vision. Standing before them for what he knew would probably be the last time, he may have wondered whether all his efforts had been in vain. "O people," he cried suddenly, "have I faithfully delivered my message to you?" There was a powerful murmur of assent from the assembled crowd: "O God, yes!" *(Allahumma na'm!)* In a touchingly human plea for reassurance, Muhammad asked the same question again—and again; and each time the words *"Allahumma na'm"* rumbled through the valley like thunder. Muhammad raised his forefinger to the heavens, and said: "O Allah, bear witness."[46]

When he returned to Medina, Muhammad began to experience incapacitating headaches and fainting attacks, but he never retired permanently to bed. He would often wrap a cloth around his aching temples and go to the mosque to lead the prayers or to address the people. One morning, he seemed to pray for an especially long time in honor of the Muslims who had died at Uhud and added: "God has given one of his servants the choice between this world and that which is with God, and he has chosen the latter." The only person who seems to have understood this reference to his imminent death was Abu Bakr, who began to weep bitterly. "Gently, gently, Abu Bakr," Muhammad said tenderly.[47]

Eventually Muhammad collapsed in the apartment of Maymunah. His wives hung lovingly over him, and noticed that he kept asking: "Where shall I be tomorrow? Where shall I be tomorrow?" and they realized that he wanted to know when he could be with 'A'isha. They agreed that he should be moved to her hut and nursed there. Muhammad lay quietly with his head in 'A'isha's lap, but people seemed to have believed that he was merely suffering from a temporary indisposition. Even though Abu Bakr repeatedly warned them that the Prophet was not long for this world, the community was in denial. When he became too ill to go to the mosque, he asked Abu Bakr to lead the prayers for him, but still he would sometimes attend salat, sitting quietly beside Abu Bakr even though he was too weak to recite the words himself.

On 12 Rabi (June 8, 632), Abu Bakr noticed during prayers that the people were distracted, and knew at once that Muhammad must have entered the mosque. He looked much better. Indeed, somebody said that they had never seen him so radiant, and a wave of joy and relief swept through the congregation. Abu Bakr instantly made ready to stand down, but Muhammad put his hands on his shoulders, pushed him gently back to the head of the community and sat down next to him until the service was over. Afterwards he went back to 'A'isha's hut and lay peacefully in her lap. He seemed so much improved that Abu Bakr asked leave to visit his wife, who lived on the other side of Medina. During the afternoon, 'Ali and 'Abbas both looked in and spread the good news that Muhammad was on the mend. As evening approached, 'A'isha felt him leaning more heavily against her than before, and he seemed to be losing consciousness. Still, she did not realize what was happening. As she said later, "It was due to my ignorance and extreme youth that the Prophet died in my arms." She heard him murmur the words: "Nay, the most Exalted Companion in Paradise"—Gabriel had come to fetch him.⁴⁸ Looking down, 'A'isha discovered that he had gone. Carefully she laid his head on the pillow and began to beat her breast, slap her face, and cry aloud in the traditional way.

When the people heard the women lamenting the dead, they hurried ashen-faced to the mosque. The news travelled quickly through the oasis and Abu Bakr hurried back to the city. He took one look at Muhammad, kissed his face, and bade him farewell. In the mosque, he found 'Umar addressing the crowds. 'Umar absolutely refused to believe that the Prophet was dead: his soul had just left his body temporarily, he argued, and he would certainly return to his people. He would be the last of them all to die. The hysteria in 'Umar's compulsive harangue must have been evident, because Abu Bakr murmured "Gently, 'Umar." But 'Umar simply could not stop talking. All that Abu Bakr could do was step forward quietly and his composure must have impressed the people, because they gradually stopped listening to 'Umar's tirade and clustered around him.

Abu Bakr reminded them that Muhammad had dedicated his life to the preaching of tawhid, the unity of God. How could they possibly imagine that he was immortal? That would be tantamount to saying that he was divine—a second god. Constantly, Muhammad had warned them against honoring him in the same way as Christians venerated Jesus: He was a mere mortal, no different from anybody else. To refuse to admit that Muhammad had died was, therefore, to deny his message. But as long as Muslims remained true to the belief that God alone was worthy of worship, Muhammad would live on in their minds. "O people, if anyone worships Muhammad, Muhammad is dead," he ended firmly. "If anyone worships God, God is alive, immortal."[49] Finally, he recited the verse that had been revealed to Muhammad after the battle of Uhud, when many of the Muslims had been shocked by the false rumor of his death: "Muhammad is naught but a Messenger; Messengers have passed away before him. Why, if he should die or is slain, will you turn upon your heels? If any man should turn about upon his heels, he will not harm God in any way; and God will recompense the thankful."[50] The verses made such an impact on the people that it was as though they were hearing them for the first time. 'Umar was completely overcome. "By God, when I heard Abu Bakr recite those words I was dumbfounded, so that my legs would not bear me and I fell to the ground knowing that the apostle was indeed dead."[51]

Muhammad had been as controversial in his dying as in his living. Very few of his followers had comprehended the full significance of his prophetic career. These fissures within the community had surfaced at Hudaybiyyah, when most of the pilgrims seem to have expected something miraculous to occur. People came to Islam for very different reasons. Many were devoted to the ideal of social justice, but not to Muhammad's ideal of nonviolence and reconciliation. The rebellious young highwaymen, who followed Abu Basir, had an entirely different agenda from the Prophet. The Bedouin tribesmen, who had not volunteered for the pilgrimage in 628, had a political rather than a religious commitment to Islam. From the very beginning, Islam was never a monolithic entity.

There is nothing surprising about this lack of unity. In the gospels, Jesus's disciples are often presented as obtuse and blind to the deeper aspect of his mission. Paradigmatic figures are usually so far ahead of their time that their contemporaries fail to understand them, and, after their deaths, the movement splinters—as Buddhism divided into Hinayana and Mahayana schools not long after the death of Siddhatta Gotama. In Islam, too, the divisions that had split the ummah during the Prophet's lifetime became even clearer after his death. Many of the Bedouin, who had never fully comprehended the religious message of the Qur'an, believed that Islam had died with Muhammad and felt free to secede from the ummah in the same way as they would renege on any treaty with a deceased chieftain. After the Prophet's death, the community was lead by his *kalifa*, his "successor." The first four caliphs were elected by the people: Abu Bakr, 'Umar, 'Uthman and 'Ali, known as the "rightly guided" (*rashidun*) caliphs. They led wars of conquest outside Arabia, but at the time these had no religious significance. Like any statesmen or generals, the rashidun were responding to a political opportunity—the disintegration of the Persian and Byzantine empires—rather than a Qur'anic imperative. The terrible civil wars that resulted in the assassinations of 'Umar, 'Uthman, 'Ali and Husayn, the Prophet's grandson, were later given a religious significance but were simply a by-product of an extraordinarily accelerated transition from a peripheral, primitive polity to the status of a major world power.

Far more surprising than this political turbulence was the Muslims' response. Their understanding of the Qur'an matured when they considered these disastrous events. Nearly every single major religious and literary development in Islam has had its origin in a desire to return to the original vision of the Prophet. Many were appalled by the lavish lifestyle of later caliphs, and tried to return to the austere vision of the early ummah. Mystics, theologians, historians, and jurists asked important questions. How could a society that killed its devout leaders claim to be guided by God? What kind of man should lead the ummah? Could rulers who lived in such luxury and condoned the poverty of the vast majority of the people be true Muslims?

These intense debates about the political leadership of the

ummah played a role in Islam that was similar to the great Christo-logical debates of the fourth and fifth centuries in Christianity. The ascetic spirituality of Sufism had its roots in this discontent. Sufis turned their back on the luxury of the court, and tried to live as aus-terely as the Prophet; they developed a mysticism modelled on his night journey and ascension to heaven. The Shi'ah, the self-styled "party of 'Ali", Muhammad's closest male relative, believed that the ummah must be led by one of 'Ali's direct descendants, since they alone had inherited the Prophet's charisma. Shiis developed a piety of protest against the injustice of mainstream Muslim society and tried to return to the egalitarian spirit of the Qur'an. Yet while these and many other movements looked back to the towering figure of Muhammad, they all took the Qur'anic vision into entirely new directions, and showed that the original revelations had the flexibility to respond to unprecedented circumstances that is essential to any great world movement. From the very start, Muslims used their Prophet as a yardstick by which to challenge their politicians and to measure the spiritual health of the ummah.

This critical spirit is needed today. Some Muslim thinkers regard the jihad against Mecca as the climax of Muhammad's career and fail to note that he eventually abjured warfare and adopted a nonviolent policy. Western critics also persist in viewing the Prophet of Islam as a man of war, and fail to see that from the very first he was opposed to the jahili arrogance and egotism that not only fuelled the aggres-sion of his time but is much in evidence in some leaders, Western and Muslim alike, today. The Prophet, whose aim was peace and practical compassion, is becoming a symbol of division and strife—a development that is not only tragic but also dangerous to the stability on which the future of our species depends.

At the end of my first attempt to write a biography of Muhammad, I quoted the prescient words of the Canadian scholar Wilfred Cantwell Smith. Writing in the mid-twentieth century shortly before the Suez Crisis, he observed that a healthy, functioning Islam had for centuries helped Muslims cultivate decent values which we in the West share, because they spring from a common tradition. Some Muslims have problems with Western modernity. They have turned against the cultures of the People of the Book, and have even begun to Islamize their new hatred of these sister faiths, which were so powerfully endorsed by the Qur'an. Cantwell Smith argued that if they are to meet the challenge of the day, Muslims must learn to understand our Western traditions and institutions, because they are not going to disappear. If Islamic societies did not do this, he maintained, they would fail the test of the twentieth century. But he pointed out that Western people also have a problem: "an inability to recognize that they share the planet not with inferiors but with equals."

> Unless Western civilization intellectually and socially, politically and economically, and the Christian church theologically, can learn to treat other men with fundamental respect, these two in their turn will have failed to come to terms with

the actualities of the twentieth century. The problems raised in this are, of course, as profound as anything that we have touched on for Islam.[52]

The brief history of the twenty-first century shows that neither side has mastered these lessons. If we are to avoid catastrophe, the Muslim and Western worlds must learn not merely to tolerate but to appreciate one another. A good place to start is with the figure of Muhammad: a complex man, who resists facile, ideologically-driven categorization, who sometimes did things that were difficult or impossible for us to accept, but who had profound genius and founded a religion and cultural tradition that was not based on the sword but whose name—"Islam"—signified peace and reconciliation.

Glossary

Terms

'abd   Slave

ahl al-beit   People of the household. Muhammad's immediate family.

ahl al-kitab   People of the Book. Usually Jews and Christians.

Allahu akhbar   "God is greater." A phrase that reminds Muslims of the transcendence and supremacy of God.

al-Rahim   The Merciful. One of the names of God.

al-Rahman   The Compassionate. One of the names of God.

Ansar   The Helpers. The Medinese Muslims.

'asibiyyah   Tribal solidarity.

ayah   (Plural: *ayat*) Sign, parable, symbol, a verse of the Qur'an.

badawah   Nomadic; hence Bedouin.

banat Allah   Daughters of Allah. See *gharaniq*.

dahr   Time, fate.

dhikr   Reminder, remembrance.

din   Religion, way of life, moral law, reckoning.

fatah   Literally "opening." Victory.

gharaniq   The three goddesses Al-Lat, Al-Uzza, and Manat. "Daughters of Allah," who were compared to beautiful "cranes".

ghazu   Acquisition raid, essential to the Bedouin economy. *Ghazi:* Warrior, raider, man of war.

hadarah   Settled life—as opposed to *badawah*.

hadith   (plural: *ahadith*) Report, a maxim or saying attributed to the Prophet.

hajj   The pilgrimage to Mecca. *Hajji:* pilgrim.

hakam   Arbitrator. Muhammad's political role in Medina.

hanif   Originally a pre-Islamic monotheist. In the Qur'an, the word refers to a person who followed the *hanifiyyah,* the pure religion of Abraham, before this split into rival sects.

haram   Sacred; forbidden—hence "sanctuary," especially the sanctuary surrounding the Kabah where all violence was prohibited.

hasab   Ancestral honor; the particular virtues of a tribe that tribesmen had inherited from their forefathers.

hijab   Curtain, veil, a covering for something precious or sacred.

hijrah   Migration, especially the Muslims' migrations to Medina.

hilm   A traditional Arab virtue which became central to Islam: forbearance, patience, mercy, tranquillity.

islam   Surrender, submission, the name eventually applied to the religion of the Qur'an.

'isra   A night journey, especially that of Muhammad to Jerusalem.

istighna'   Haughty self-reliance, aggressive independence and self-sufficiency.

jahiliyyah   Traditionally translated "Time of Ignorance," and used to apply to the pre-Islamic period in Arabia, but in the Muslim sources its primary meaning is violent and explosive irascibility, arrogance, tribal chauvinism.

jahim   An obscure word, usually translated "raging fire." Hell.

jihad   Struggle, effort, endeavour.

jilbab   A garment, cloak, or covering.

jinni   (plural: *jinn*) "Unseen being," usually one of the sprites who haunted the Arabian desert, inspired poets, and led people astray; also stranger, a person hitherto "unseen."

Kabah   Literally, cube. The granite shrine in the Haram, dedicated to Allah.

kafir   (Plural: *kafirun*) Traditionally translated "unbeliever." More accurately it refers to somebody who ungratefully and aggressively rejects Allah and refuses to acknowledge his dependence on the Creator.

kalifa   The successor of Muhammad, the caliph.

karim   Generous hero; the Bedouin ideal.

kufr   Ingratitude; insolence.

kunya   Honorary title assumed by a man after the birth of his first son; e.g. Abu Bakr, the father of Bakr.

layla   Night; also, a woman's name.

layla al-qadr   Night of destiny; the night when Muhammad received the first revelation from God.

masjid   A place for prostration; later, mosque.

mirbad   A place for drying dates.

mu'min   Those who faithfully live up to the Muslim ideal.

munafiq   (Plural: *munafiqun*) Waverer; hypocrite; the term applied to an uncommitted Muslim who followed Ibn Ubbay.

muruwah   The chivalric code of the Bedouin, comprising loyalty to the tribe, courage, endurance, generosity, and reverence for the tribal ancestors.

muslim   A person who has surrendered his or her entire being to God; who has made the act of *islam.*

nadhir   A messenger who brings a warning to his people.

nasr   Help, including military support.

qiblah   The direction of prayer.

Qur'an   "Recitation." The scripture that was revealed to Muhammad by God.

rashidun   The "rightly guided" ones; the first four caliphs.

ruh   Spirit. In the Qur'an, the divine spirit of revelation.

sakinah   The spirit of peace and serenity.

salam   Peace; often used by Muslims as a greeting.

salat   The ritual worship performed five times a day by Muslims.

salihat   The works of justice prescribed by the Qur'an.

saraya   A wife with slave status, but whose children are free.

sayyid   Chief of a clan or tribe.

shahadah   The Muslim declaration of faith: "I bear witness that there is no god but Allah and that Muhammad is his prophet."

shari'ah   Originally, the path to the watering hole. The lifeline of a nomadic tribe; later applied to the body of Muslim law.

shaytan   A "satan." A tempter who could be a human being or one of the *jinn*, who leads people astray and inspires facile, empty desires.

shirk   Idolatry, associating other beings with God, putting other deities or purely human values on the same level as Allah. The cardinal Muslim sin.

sunnah   A path, a way of life.

suq   Market, trade fair.

surah   A chapter of the Qur'an.

taqarrush   Acquisition, gaining. Perhaps the origin of "Quraysh."

taqwa'   Mindfulness; an attitude of sensitivity to and consciousness of God.

tawaf   The seven ritual circumambulations around the Kabah.

tawhid   "Making one", the unity of God, realized in the integration of the human person.

tazakka   Purification, refinement. An early name for the religion of Islam.

ummah   Community.

umrah   The Lesser Pilgrimage. The rites of the *hajj* that were performed within the city of Mecca, excluding those performed in the surrounding countryside.

yawm ad-din   Day of reckoning; moment of truth.

zakat Literally "purification" Alms; a charitable donation to the needy. One of the essential practices of Islam.

zalim Outsider; a person who is abhorred because he does not belong to the tribe.

Places

'Abd Shams The neighborhood of the Qurayshan clan of 'Abd Shams in Mecca.

'Aqabah The gully outside Mecca where Muhammad first met with pilgrims from Yathrib.

'Arafat A mountain sixteen miles east of Mecca; one of the stations of the *hajj*, where pilgrims made an all-night vigil.

Badr A watering hole on the Red Sea coast, where the Muslims achieved their first victory over the Meccan army.

Hijaz A region in the northern Arabian steppes.

Hira' A mountain outside Mecca, where Muhammad received the first revelation in about 610.

Hudaybiyyah A well within the confines of the Meccan sanctuary, where Muhammad made a peace treaty with the Quraysh in 628.

Khaybar An agricultural settlement of Jewish tribes, north of Medina.

Marwah A hill to the east of the Kabah; during the *hajj*, pilgrims would run seven times between Marwah and Safe.

Mecca The commercial city ruled by the Quraysh; the birthplace of Muhammad.

Medina   The name given by the Muslims to the settlement of
   Yathrib; the city of the Prophet.

Mina   A valley about five miles east of Mecca; one of the stations
   of the *hajj*.

Mu'tah   A town near the Syrian border, where the Muslim army
   suffered a severe military defeat.

Muzdalifah   One of the stations of the *hajj*; a valley between Mina
   and 'Arafat, thought originally to have been the home of the
   thunder god.

Nakhlah   An oasis to the south-east of Mecca, where the goddess
   Al-Uzzah had her shrine and sanctuary.

Qudhayd   A city on the Red Sea coast, where the goddess Manat
   had her shrine and sanctuary.

Safa   A hill to the east of the Kabah; during the *hajj*, pilgrims
   would run between Safa and Marwah.

Sana'a   A city in southern Arabia; now the capital of Yemen.

Ta'if   An agricultural colony to the south-east of Mecca; the site
   of the sanctuary of the goddess Al-Lat and home of the tribe of
   Thaqif. Ta'if supplied Mecca with most of its food, and many of
   the Quraysh had summer homes there.

Uhud   A mountain to the north of Medina; the Meccans inflicted a severe defeat over the Muslim army on the adjoining
   plain.

'Ukaz   The site of one of the great trade fairs, where a poetry
   contest was held each year.

Yathrib   An agricultural settlement, some 250 miles north of

Mecca, populated by Arabs and Jewish tribes. After the *hijrah,* it became known as Medina, the city of the Prophet.

Zamzam   The sacred spring in the Meccan Haram.

People

'Abdullah ibn Ubayy   A chief of the Khazraj clan in Medina, who led the opposition to Muhammad.

'Abdullah ibn 'Abd al-Muttalib   The father of Muhammad, who died before he was born.

Abdullah ibn Jahsh   The cousin of Muhammad; brother of his wife Zaynab, and Ubaydallah, the *hanif.*

'Abbas ibn 'Abd al-Muttalib   The uncle of Muhammad.

'Abd al-Muttalib   Muhammad's grandfather.

Abu l-'As ar-Rabi   The husband of Muhammad's daughter, Zaynab, who resisted conversion to Islam for many years.

Abu Ja'rir at-Tabari   Historian and biographer of Muhammad.

Abu l-Hakam ibn Hisham   See Abu Jahl.

Abu Bakr   A close and trusted friend of Muhammad; one of the first converts to Islam; the father of 'A'isha, the beloved wife of the Prophet.

Abu Bara'   Chief of the Bedouin tribe of 'Amir; Muhammad married his daughter Zaynab bint Khuzaymah after the battle of Uhud.

Abu Jahl   "Father of Insolence," the nickname given by the Muslims to Abu l-Hakam; the most virulent of Muhammad's early opponents.

Abu Lahab ibn 'Abd al-Muttalib   The half-brother of Abu Talib; an early opponent of Muhammad. After Abu Talib's death, he became the chief of the clan of Hashim.

Abu Sufyan ibn Harb   Chief of the Qurayshan clan of 'Abd Shams; a leading opponent of Islam.

Abu Talib ibn 'Abd al-Muttalib   Muhammad's uncle, guardian, and protector.

'A'isha bint Abi Bakr   Daughter of Abu Bakr; Muhammad's beloved young wife.

Al-Muttalib   One of the Meccan clans, closely related to Hashim, Muhammad's clan.

'Ali ibn Abi Talib   Abu Talib's son; the ward of Muhammad and Khadijah. He married Fatimah, the Prophet's daughter.

Aminah bint Wahb   Muhammad's mother; she died during his infancy.

Amir   A Meccan clan.

'Asad   The Meccan clan to which Khadijah belonged.

Aslam   A Bedouin tribe.

'Amr ibn al-'As   A leading warrior in the Meccan army and an opponent of Islam.

Anas ibn Malik   A friend of Muhammad; present when the Verses of the Hijab were revealed.

Aws   One of the Arab tribes in Medina.

Bani Qaylah   "The Sons of Qaylah." The Arab tribe that migrated from southern Arabia to Yathrib during the sixth century and later split into the Aws and Khazraj.

Bara' ibn Mar'ar   A chief of Khazraj; the patron of Muhammad during the Pledge of War (622).

Bilal   An Abyssinian slave who converted to Islam; he became the first *muezzin* to call the Muslims to prayer.

Budayl ibn Warqa   Chief of the Bedouin tribe of Khuza'ah.

Fatimah bint Muhammad   The youngest daugther of Muhammad and Khadijah; the wife of 'Ali.

Gabriel   The angel or spirit of the divine revelation.

Ghassan   An Arab tribe on the Byzantine border that had converted to Christianity and become an ally of Byzantium.

Ghatafan   A Bedouin tribe, based in the desert region east of Medina, allied to Ibn Ubayy and the opponents of Muhammad.

Hafsah bint 'Umar   The daughter of 'Umar ibn al-Khattab; the wife of Muhammad; a special friend of 'A'isha.

Hamzah ibn al-Muttalib   One of Muhammad's uncles; a warrior of prodigious strength, who converted to Islam and died at the battle of Uhud.

Hasan ibn 'Ali   The Prophet's grandson, the older son of 'Ali and Fatimah.

Hashim   The Meccan clan to which Muhammad belonged.

Hind bint Abi Umayyah   See Umm Salamah.

Hind bint 'Utbah   The wife of Abu Sufyan; an implacable enemy of Muhammad.

Hubal   A god probably imported from the Nabatean region and venerated in Mecca; his stone effigy stood beside the Kabah.

Hulays ibn 'Alaqamah   Chief of the Bedouin tribe of al-Harith.

Husayn ibn 'Ali   The younger son of 'Ali and Fatimah.

Huyay ibn Akhtab   Chief of the Jewish tribe of Nadir.

Ibn Dughunnah   A Bedouin chieftain confederated to the Quraysh; he became the protector of Abu Bakr.

Ibn Ishaq   Muhammad ibn Ishaq; the first biographer of Muhammad.

Ibn Sa'd   Muhammad ibn Sa'd; Muslim historian and biographer of the Prophet.

Ibn Ubayy   See 'Abdullah ibn Ubayy.

'Ikrimah   Son of Abu Jahl; one of the leaders of the Meccan opposition to Muhammad.

Ja'far ibn Abi Talib   Cousin of Muhammad.

Jumah   A Meccan clan of Quraysh.

Jurham   A Bedouin tribe.

Juwayriyyah bint al-Harith   Daughter of a Bedouin chieftain; wife of Muhammad.

Khadijah bint al-Khuwaylid   Muhammad's first wife.

Khalid ibn al-Walid   One of Mecca's outstanding warriors; opponent of Muhammad for many years.

Khazraj   One of the Arab tribes in Medina.

Khuza'ah   One of the Bedouin tribes that had controlled the Meccan sanctuary before the arrival of the Quraysh.

Kilab   An Arab tribe allied to the Jewish tribe of Quraysh.

Makhzum   A Meccan clan of Quraysh.

Maryam   An Egyptian Christian; *saraya* wife of Muhammad.

Maymunah bint al-Harith   Sister of 'Abbas; married to Muhammad during the Lesser Pilgrimage of 629.

Mus'ab ibn 'Umayr   The Muslim sent to instruct the Medinese before the *hijrah*.

Mu'tim ibn 'Adi   Muhammad's protector during his last years in Mecca before the *hijrah*.

Nadir   A powerful Jewish tribe of Medina opposed to Muhammad; exiled from Medina after an assassination attempt; took refuge in Khaybar. Nadiri: a member of Nadir.

Qaswa'   Muhammad's favorite camel.

Qaynuqa'   A Jewish tribe in Medina that controlled the market; they rebelled against Muhammad and were expelled from Medina.

Quraysh   Muhammad's tribe, rulers of Mecca; *Adj.* Qurayshan; Qurayshi; a member of the tribe.

Qurayzah   A Jewish tribe that collaborated with Mecca during the Battle of Trench; the men were executed, the women and children sold into slavery.

Qusayy ibn Kilab   The founder of the tribe of Quraysh.

Ruqayyah bint Muhammad   Daughter of Khadijah and Muhammad; married to 'Uthman ibn' Affan.

Sa'd ibn Mu'adh   A chieftain of the Aws tribe in Medina.

Sa'd ibn 'Ubadah   A chieftain of Khazraj tribe in Medina.

Safiyyah bint Huyay   Muhammad's Jewish wife, married to him after the conquest of Khaybar.

Safwan ibn al-Mu'attal   A friend of 'A'isha; Muhammad's Medinese opponents spread slanderous rumors about their relationship.

Safwan ibn Umayyah   One of the leading members of the opposition to Muhammad in Mecca.

Sawdah bint Zam'ah   Wife of Muhammad; the cousin and sister-in-law of Suhayl ibn 'Amr.

Suhayl ibn 'Amr   Chief of the clan of Amir in Mecca; a devout pagan; a leading member of the opposition to Muhammad.

Thalabah   One of the twenty Jewish tribes of Yathrib/Medina.

Thaqif   An Arab tribe, settled in Ta'if; the allies of the Quraysh; opponents of Muhammad.

'Ubaydallah ibn al-Harith   An experienced Qurayshan warrior who converted to Islam.

'Ubaydallah ibn Jahsh   Cousin of Muhammad; a *hanif* who converted to Christianity.

Umamah bint 'Abu l-'As   The granddaughter of Muhammad; the daughter of Zaynab bint Muhammad.

'Umar ibn al-Khattab   The nephew of Abu Jahl; at first passionately opposed to Muhammad, but later became one of his closest companions.

Umayyah   A powerful Meccan clan of Quraysh.

Ummayah ibn Khalaf   Chief of the Meccan clan of Jumah; an inveterate opponent of Muhammad.

Umm Habibah   Daughter of Abu Sufyan; one of the émigrés to Abyssinia; married to Muhammad on her return.

Umm Han' bint Abi Talib   Muhammad's cousin.

Umm Kulthum bint Muhammad   Daughter of Muhammad and Khadijah; married 'Uthman ibn 'Affan after the death of Ruqayyah.

Umm Salamah bint Abi Umayyah   One of the most sophisticated and intelligent of Muhammad's wives.

'Urwah ibn Mas'ud   A member of Thaqif; an ally of the Quraysh and an opponent of Muhammad.

'Utbah ibn Rabi'ah   A leading member of the Meccan clan of 'Abd Shams, with a summer home in Ta'if; an opponent of Muhammad.

'Uthman ibn 'Affan   One of the earliest converts, with family connections to some of the most powerful clans in Mecca; he became Muhammad's son-in-law.

Waraqah Ibn Nawfal   Cousin of Khadijah; a *hanif* who had converted to Christianity.

Zayd ibn al-Harith   The adopted son of Muhammad and Khadijah; married to Zayab bint Jahsh, Muhammad's cousin.

Zayd ibn 'Amr   One of the early *hanifs*, who was driven out of Mecca because of his stinging criticism of the traditional pagan religion; the uncle of 'Umar ibn al-Khattab.

Zaynab bint Jahsh   Muhammad's cousin; married first to Zayd ibn al-Harith; after their divorce, she married Muhammad.

Zaynab bint Khuzaymah   Muhammad's wife; the daughter of the chief of the Bedouin tribe of 'Amir; she died eight months after her marriage to the Prophet.

Zaynab bint Muhammad   The daughter of Muhammad and
   Khadijah; the wife of 'Abu al-'As; a devout pagan who for many
   years resisted conversion to Islam.

Notes

1. *Mecca*

1. Tor Andrae, *Muhammad: The Man and His Faith,* trans. Theophil Menzel (London, 1936), 59.
2. Quoted in R. A. Nicholson, *A Literary History of the Arabs* (Cambridge, 1953), 83.
3. Toshihiko Izutsu, *Ethico-Religious Concepts in the Qur'an* (Montreal and Kingston, ON, 2002), 46.
4. Ibid., 63.
5. Labid ibn 'Rabi'ah, *Mu'allaqah,* 5.81, in Izutsu, *Ethico-Religious Concepts,* 63; cf. Qur'an 2:170, 43:22–24.
6. Izutsu, *Ethico-Religious Concepts,* 72.
7. Ibid., 29.

8. Zuhayr ibn 'Abi Salma, verses 38–39 in Izutsu, *Ethico-Religious Concepts*, 84.
9. Nicholson, *Literary History*, 93.
10. Mohammad A. Bamyeh, *The Social Origins of Islam: Mind, Economy, Discourse* (Minneapolis, 1999), 17–20.
11. Ibid., 30.
12. Ibid., 11–12.
13. Ibid., 38.
14. Qur'an 105.
15. Johannes Sloek, *Devotional Language,* trans. Henrick Mossin (Berlin and New York, 1996), 89–90.
16. Bamyeh, *Social Origins of Islam*, 32.
17. Ibid., 43.
18. Muhammad ibn Ishaq, *Sirat Rasul Allah*, 120, in A. Guillaume, trans., *The Life of Muhammad: A Translation of Ishaq's* Sirat Rasul Allah (London, 1955); cf. Leila Ahmed, *Women and Gender in Islam* (New Haven and London, 1992), 42.
19. Ibid., 155, Guillaume translation.
20. Qur'an 103:2–3.
21. Qur'an 6:70, 7:51.
22. Wilhelm Schmidt, *The Origin of the Idea of God* (New York, 1912), *passim*.
23. Qur'an 10:22–24, 24:61, 63, 39:38, 43:87, 106:1–3.
24. Izutsu, *God and Man in the Koran, Semantics of the Koranic Weltanschauung* (Tokyo, 1964), 93–101, 124–129.

25. F. E. Peters, *The Hajj: The Muslim Pilgrimage to Mecca and the Holy Places* (Princeton, 1994), 24–27.

26. Ibn al-Kalbi, *The Book of Idols* in Peters, *Hajj,* 29.

27. Bamyeh, *Social Origins of Islam,* 22–24.

28. Ibid., 79–80; Reza Aslan, *No god but God, The Origins, Evolution, and Future of Islam* (New York and London, 2005), 9–13.

29. Genesis 16.

30. Flavius Josephus, *The Antiquities of the Jews,* 1.12.2.

31. Bamyeh, *Social Origins of Islam,* 25–27.

32. Psalm 135:5.

33. Bamyeh, *Social Origins of Islam,* 89–144; Aslan, *No god but God,* 13–15; Izutsu, *God and Man,* 107–18.

34. Ibn Ishaq, *Sirat Rasul Allah,* 143, in Guillaume, *Life of Muhammad.*

35. Ibid., 145, in Guillaume, *Life of Muhammad.*

36. Peters, *Hajj,* 39–40.

37. Izutsu, *God and Man,* 148.

38. Ibn Ishaq, *Sirat Rasul Allah,* 151, in Guillaume, *Life of Muhammad,* 105.

39. Qur'an 96 in Michael Sells, ed. and trans., *Approaching the Qur'an: The Early Revelations* (Ashland, OR, 1999). Muhammad Asad translates lines 6–8: "Verily man becomes grossly overweening whenever he believes himself to be self-sufficient: for, behold, unto thy Sustainer all must return."

40. Qur'an 53:5–9, Sells translation.

41. Ibn Ishaq, *Sirat Rasul Allah*, 153, in Guillaume, *Life of Muhammad*.

42. Ibid.

43. Ibid., 154.

44. Qur'an 21:91, 19:16–27. Sells, *Approaching the Qur'an*, 187–93.

45. Qur'an 97, Sells translation.

46. Rudolf Otto, *The Idea of the Holy: An Inquiry into the Non Rational Factor in the Idea of the Divine and its relation to the rational*, trans. John W. Harvey, 2nd ed., (London, Oxford and New York, 1950), 12–40.

47. Qur'an 93, Sells translation.

2. *Jahiliyyah*

1. This was noted by the seventh century Meccan historian Ibn Shifan al-Zuhri, who is quoted in W. Montgomery Watt, *Muhammad at Mecca* (Oxford, 1953), 87.

2. Muhammad ibn Ishaq, *Sirat Rasul Allah*, 161, in A. Guillaume, trans. and ed., *The Life of Muhammad: A Translation of Ishaq's* Sirat Rasul Allah (London, 1955), 115.

3. Muhammad ibn Sa'd, *Kitab al-Tabaqat al-Kabir*, 4.1.68, in Martin Lings, *Muhammad: His Life Based on the Earliest Sources* (London, 1983), 47.

4. Ibn Sa'd, 3.1.37, *Kitab at-Tabaqat*, in Lings, *Muhammad*, 47.

5. Qur'an 27:45–46, 28:4.

6. Jalal al-Din Suyuti, *al-itqan fi'ulum al-aq'ran*, quoted in Maxime

Rodinson, *Mohammed*, trans. Anne Carter (London, 1971), 74.

7. Bukhari, *Hadith* 1.3, in Lings, *Muhammad*, 44–45.

8. Qur'an 20:114, 75:16–18.

9. Michael Sells, ed. and trans., *Approaching the Qur'an: The Early Revelations* (Ashland, OR, 1999), xvi.

10. Sells, *Approaching the Qur'an*, 183–84.

11. Mircea Eliade, *Yoga: Immorality and Freedom*, trans. Willard Trask (London, 1958), 56.

12. Sells, *Approaching the Qur'an*, 183–204. See also Qur'an 81:8–9.

13. See Qur'an 82:17–18, 83:8–9, 19.

14. Sells, *Approaching the Qur'an*, xliii.

15. Qur'an 81:1–6, 14, in Sells, *Approaching the Qur'an*.

16. Qur'an 99:6–9, Sells translation.

17. Qur'an 90:13–16, Sells translation.

18. Qur'an 81:26, Sells translation.

19. Qur'an 88:21–22.

20. Qur'an 88:17–20, Sells translation.

21. Watt, *Muhammad at Mecca*, 68.

22. Qur'an 26:214.

23. Qur'an 17:26–27.

24. Abu Ja'rir at-Tabari, *Ta'rikh ar-Rasul wa'l Muluk*, 1171 in Guillaume, *Life of Muhammad*, 117–118.

25. Qur'an 83:4, 37:12–19.

26. Qur'an 45:23, 36:77–83.

27. Qur'an 83:10–12.

28. Qur'an 6:108, 27:45, 10:71–72. Mohammed A. Bamyeh, *The Social Origins of Islam, Mind, Economy, Discourse* (Minneapolis, 1999), 180–184.

29. Qur'an 10:72.

30. Wilfred Cantwell Smith, *Faith and Belief* (Princeton, 1979), 44–46; Toshihiko Izutsu, *Ethico-Religious Concepts in the Qur'an* (Montreal and Kingston, ON, 2002), 132–133.

31. Tor Andrae, *Muhammad: The Man and His Faith,* trans. Theophil Menzel (London: 1936), 22–35; W. Montgomery Watt, *Muhammad's Mecca: History in the Qur'an* (Edinburgh, 1988), 69–73; Watt, *Muhammad at Mecca,* 103–109; Bamyeh, *Social Origins of Islam,* 208–9.

32. Ibn Sa'd, *Kitab at-Tabaqat* 8i, 137, in Bamyeh, *Social Origins of Islam,* 208.

33. Tabari, *Ta'rikh ar-Rasul,* 1192, in Guillaume, *Life of Muhammad,* 165.

34. Qur'an 53:12.

35. Qur'an 53:26.

36. Tabari, *Ta'rikh ar-Rasul,* 1192, in Guillaume, *Life of Muhammad,* 166.

37. Ibn Sa'd, *Kitab at-Tabaqat,* 137, in Andrae, *Muhammad,* 22.

38. Tabari, *Ta'rikh ar-Rasul,* 1192, in Guillaume, *Life of Muhammad,* 166.

39. Qur'an 22:52.

40. Qur'an 53:19–23, in Muhammad Asad, trans. and ed., *The Message of the Qur'an* (Gibraltar, 1980).

41. Qur'an 39:23, translation by Izutsu, *Ethico-Religious Concepts*, 197.

42. Qur'an 59:21, Asad translation.

43. Qur'an 29:17, 10:18, 39:43.

44. Qur'an 112, Sells translation.

45. Reza Aslan, *No god but God: The Origins, Evolution and Future of Islam* (London and New York, 2005), 43–46.

46. Ibn Ishaq, *Sirat Rasul Allah*, 167–8, in Guillaume, *Life of Muhammad*, 119.

47. Qur'an 17:46, 39:45.

48. Qur'an 38:6.

49. Qur'an 38:4–5.

50. Qur'an 41:6.

51. Qur'an 80:1–10.

52. Izutsu, *Ethico-Religious Concepts*, 66; Cantwell Smith, *Faith and Belief*, 39–40.

53. Qur'an 29:61–63, 2:89, 27:14.

54. Qur'an 17:23–24, 46:15. Asad translation.

55. Izutsu, *Ethico-Religious Concepts*, 127–57.

56. Qur'an 7:75–76, 39:59, 31:17–18, 23:45–47, 38:71–75.

57. Qur'an 15:94–96, 21:36, 18:106, 40:4–5, 68:56, 22:8–9.

58. Qur'an 41:3–5, 83:14, 2:6–7.

59. Izutsu, *Ethico-Religious Concepts*, 28–45.

60. Ibid., 28.

61. Ibid., 68–69, Qur'an 14:47, 39:37, 15:79, 30:47, 44:16.

62. Qur'an 90:13–17.

63. Qur'an 25:63, Asad translation.

64. Qur'an 111. This is the only occasion when the Qur'an mentions one of Muhammad's enemies by name.

65. Ibn Ishaq, *Sirat Rasul Allah,* 183–4 in Guillaume, *Life of Muhammad,* 130–31.

66. Ibid., in Guillaume, *Life of Muhammad,* 132.

67. Ibn Ishaq, *Sirat Rasul Allah,* 227, in Guillaume, *Life of Muhammad,* 157.

68. Ibid., 228, in Guillaume, *Life of Muhammad,* 158.

69. Aslan, *No god but God,* 46.

70. Qur'an 11:100.

71. Qur'an 2:100, 13:37, 16:101, 17:41, 17:86.

72. Qur'an 109, Sells translation.

73. Qur'an 2:256, Asad translation.

3. Hijrah

1. Muhammad ibn Ishaq, *Sirat Rasul Allah,* 278, in A. Guillaume, trans. and ed., *The Life of Muhammad* (London, 1955), 169–70.

2. Ibid., 280, in Guillaume, *Life of Muhammad,* 193.

3. Qur'an 46:29–32, 72:1, in Muhammad Asad, trans. and ed., *The Message of the Qur'an* (Gibraltar, 1980). This is Asad's explanation of this incident, given in the textual notes that accompany this passage, which he admits is tentative.

4. Qur'an 17:1, Asad translation.

5. Muhammad ibn Jarir at-Tabari, *Ta'rikh ar Rasul wa'l Muluk,*

2210, Muhammad A. Bamyeh, *The Social Origins of Islam: Mind, Economy, Discourse* (Minneapolis, 1999), 144–45.

6. Qur'an 53:15–18 in Michael Sells, trans. and ed., *Approaching the Qur'an; The Early Revelations* (Ashland, OR, 1999).

7. Sells, ibid., xvii–xviii.

8. Ibn Ishaq, *Sirat Rasul Allah,* 271, in Guillaume, *Life of Muhammad.*

9. Qur'an 3:84, cf. 2:136, Asad translation.

10. Toshihiko Izutsu, *Ethico-Religious Concepts in the Qur'an* (Montreal and Kingston, ON, 2002), 189.

11. Qur'an 3:85, Asad translation.

12. Qur'an 12:111.

13. Qur'an 5:69, Asad translation.

14. Qur'an 5:48, Asad translation.

15. Qur'an 24:35, Asad translation.

16. Martin Lings, *Muhammad: His Life Based on the Earliest Sources* (London: Islamic Society Texts, 1983), 57, 105–111; W. Montgomery Watt, *Muhammad at Mecca* (Oxford, 1953), 141–49; Watt, *Muhammad at Medina* (Oxford, 1956), 173–231.

17. Reza Aslan, *No god but God: The Origins, Evolution and Future of Islam* (London and New York, 2005), 54; Gordon Newby, *A History of the Jews in Arabia* (Columbia, SC, 1988), 75–79, 84–85; Moshe Gil, "Origin of the Jews of Yathrib," *Jerusalem Studies in Arabic and Islam* (1984).

18. Muhammad ibn 'Umar al-Waqidi, *Kitab al-Maghazi* in Aslan, *No god but God,* 54.

19. Ibn Ishaq, 287, in Guillaume, *Life of Muhammad.*

20. Ibid., 289, in Bamyeh, *Social Origins of Islam,* 153–54.

21. Ibid., 291–2, in Guillaume, *Life of Muhammad.*

22. Bamyeh, *Social Origins of Islam,* 153–3.

23. Qur'an 5:5–7; cf. Acts of Apostles 15:19–21, 29.

24. Qur'an 10:47.

25. Qur'an 8:30, 27:48–51.

26. Qur'an 60:1, 47–13.

27. W. Montgomery Watt, *Muhammad's Mecca: History of the Qur'an* (Edinburgh, 1988), 101–6; *Muhammad at Mecca,* 149–51.

28. Watt, *Muhammad's Mecca,* 25.

29. Izutsu, *Ethico-Religious Concepts,* 56.

30. Ibn Ishaq, *Sirat Rasul Allah,* 297, in Guillaume, *Life of Muhammad.*

31. Ibid., 304–5, in Guillaume, *Life of Muhammad.*

32. Bamyeh, *Social Origins of Islam,* 216–217.

33. Aslan, *No god but God,* 56–59.

34. Ibn Ishaq, *Sirat Rasul Allah,* in Guillaume, *Life of Muhammad.*

35. Qur'an 9:40.

36. Clinton Bennet, "Islam," in Jean Holm with John Bowker, eds, *Sacred Place* (London, 1994), 88–89; Fatima Mernissi, *Women and Islam: An Historical and Theological Enquiry,* trans. Mary Jo Lakeland (Oxford, 1991), 106–108.

37. Ibn Ishaq, *Sirat Rasul Allah,* 247, in Guillaume, *Life of Muhammad,* 236.

38. Ibid., 414, in Guillaume, *Life of Muhammad.*

39. Bamyeh, *Social Origins of Islam,* 218.

40. Qur'an 8:72–73, Asad translation.

41. Ibn Ishaq, *Sirat Rasul Allah,* 341, in Guillaume, *Life of Muhammad,* 232.

42. Qur'an 43:37–43, Asad translation.

43. Ibn Ishaq, *Sirat Rasul Allah,* 386, translation in Izutsu, *Ethico-Religious Concepts,* 29.

44. Qur'an 4:137, Asad translation.

45. Qur'an 2:8–15, Asad translation.

46. Ibn Ishaq, *Sirat Rasul Allah,* 341, in Guillaume, *Life of Muhammad.*

47. Watt, *Muhammad at Medina,* 201–2.

48. D. S. Margoliouth, *The Relations between Arabs and Israelites Prior to the Rise of Islam* (London, 1924); Salo Wittmayer Baron, *A Social and Religious History of the Jews* (New York: Columbia University Press, 1964), 3:261; Hannah Rahman, "The Conflict between the Prophet and the Opposition in Medina," *Der Islam* (1985); Moshe Gil, "The Medinan Opposition to the Prophet," *Jerusalem Studies in Arabic and Islam* (1987).

49. S. N. Goitein, *Jews and Arabs* (New York, 1960), 63; Newby, *History of the Jews,* 78–90; Aslan, *No god but God,* 97–98.

50. David J. Helperin, "The Ibn Sayyad Traditions and the Legend of al-Dajjal," *Journal of the American Oriental Society* (1976).

51. Ibn Ishaq, *Sirat Rasul Allah.*, 362, in Guillaume, *Life of Muhammad.*

52. Qur'an 6:151.

53. Qur'an 2:111–113, 120.

54. Qur'an 2:116, 19:88–92, 10:68, 5:73–77, 116–118.

55. Qur'an 5:73.

56. Qur'an 3:115, Asad translation.

57. Qur'an 2:67–68, Asad translation.

58. Qur'an 3:65.

59. Qur'an 3:67, in Arthur J. Arberry, trans. and ed., *The Koran Interpreted* (Oxford, 1964).

60. Qur'an 6:159, Asad translation.

61. Qur'an 6:161–3.

62. Qur'an 2:144, Asad translation.

63. Qur'an 2:150, Asad translation.

4. *Jihad*

1. Muhammad A. Bamyeh, *The Social Origins of Islam: Mind, Economy, Discourse* (Minneapolis, 1999), 198.

2. W. Montgomery Watt, *Muhammad at Medina* (Oxford, 1956), 2–5.

3. Qur'an 2:216.

4. Qur'an 22:36–40, in Muhammad Asad, trans., *The Message of the Qur'an* (Gibraltar, 1980).

5. Qur'an 2:190.

6. Watt, *Muhammad at Medina*, 6–8; Bamyeh, *Social Origins of Islam*, 198–99; Marshall G. S. Hodgson, *The Venture of Islam: Conscience and History in a World Civilization*, 3 vols (Chicago

and London, 1974), 1:175–76; Tor Andrae, *Muhammad: The Man and His Faith,* trans. Theophil Menzel (London, 1936), 195–201.

7. Qur'an 2:217, Asad translation.

8. Bamyeh, *Social Origins of Islam,* 200, 231; Andrae, *Muhammad,* 203–6; Watt, *Muhammad at Medina,* 11–20; Martin Lings, *Mohammad: His Life Based on the Earliest Sources* (London, 1983), 138–59.

9. Muhammad Ibn Ishaq, *Sirat Rasul Allah,* 435, in A. Guillaume, trans. and ed., *The Life of Muhammad: A Translation of Ishaq's Sirat Rasul Allah* (London, 1955).

10. Ibid.

11. Qur'an 8:5–9.

12. Muhammad Ibn Jarir at-Tabari, *Ta'rikh ar-Rasul wa'l Muluk,* in Fatima Mernissi, *Women in Islam: An Historical and Theological Enquiry,* trans. Mary Jo Lakeland (Oxford, 1991), 90.

13. Qur'an 8:8.

14. Ibn Ishaq, *Sirat Rasul Allah,* 442, in Guillaume, *Life of Muhammad.*

15. Qur'an 47:5.

16. Qur'an 3:147–48, 8:16–17, 61:5.

17. Qur'an 2:193–194.

18. Qur'an 8:62–63.

19. Qur'an 5:45, Asad translation.

20. Qur'an 4:90.

21. Reza Aslan, *No god but God: The Origins, Evolution and Future*

of Islam (New York and London, 2005), 89–90; Watt, *Muhammad at Medina*, 225–43.

22. Nabia Abbott, *Aishah, the Beloved of Muhammad* (Chicago, 1992), 67.

23. Mernissi, *Women and Islam*, 106–11.

24. Muhammad al-Bukhari, *Al-Sahih* (Beirut, 1978); Mernissi, *Women and Islam*, 142–3; Leila Ahmed, *Women and Gender in Islam* (New Haven and London, 1992), 52–53.

25. Ibn Ishaq, *Sirat Raszul Allah*, 543, in Guillaume, *Life of Muhammad*.

26. Aslan, *No god but God*, 89–90; Lings, *Muhammad*, 160–62; Andrae, *Muhammad*, 207; Watt, *Muhammad at Medina*, 190–210.

27. Ibn Ishaq, *Sirat Rasul Allah*, 296, in Guillaume, *Life of Muhammad*.

28. M. J. Kister, "Al-Hira: Some Notes on its Relations with Arabia," *Jerusalem Studies in Arabic and Islam* 6 (1985).

29. Lings, *Muhammad*, 170–97; Andrae, *Muhammad*, 210–2213; Watt, *Muhammad at Medina*, 20–30.

30. Ibn Ishaq, 717, in Guillaume, *Life of Muhammad*.

31. Qur'an 4:3–3, Asad translation.

32. Watt, *Muhammad at Medina*, 272–83, 289–93; cf. Ahmed, *Women and Gender in Islam*, 43–44, 52.

33. Mernissi, *Women and Islam*, 123, 182.

34. Qur'an 24:33, in Arthur J. Arberry, *The Koran Intepreted* (Oxford, 1964).

35. Mernissi, *Women and Islam,* 162–3; Ahmed, *Women and Gender in Islam,* 53.

36. Lings, *Muhammad,* 203–4; Watt, *Muhammad at Medina,* 185, 211–17; Aslan, *No god but God,* 90–91; Bamyeh, *Social Origins of Islam,* 201–2.

37. Lings, *Muhammad,* 207–8.

38. Qur'an 24:53, 32:29, 47:35, 46. Watt, *Muhammad at Medina,* 231–4.

39. Qur'an 4:102; Lings, *Muhammad,* 208–10; Mernissi, *Women and Islam,* 163–7.

40. Lings, *Muhammad,* 21–212; Mernissi, *Women and Islam,* 153–4, 172.

41. Qur'an 49:2, 4–5.

42. Muhammad ibn Sa'd, *Tabaqat al-kubra* (Beirut, n.d.), 8:174; Mernissi, *Women and Islam,* 172.

43. Lings, *Muhammad,* 107–8; Mernissi, *Women and Islam,* 174.

44. Tabari, *Tafsir* (Cairo, n.d.), 22:10; Mernissi, *Women and Islam,* 115–31. In some versions, all Muhammad's wives, not simply Umm Salamah, take the initiative.

45. Qur'an 33:35.

46. Qur'an 4:37.

47. Qur'an 4:23.

48. Qur'an 2:225–240, 65:1–70.

49. Tabari, *Tafsir,* 9:235; Mernissi, *Women and Islam,* 131–32; Ahmed, *Women and Gender in Islam,* 53.

50. Qur'an 4:19.

51. Tabari, *Tafsir,* 8:261; Mernissi, *Women and Islam,* 132.

52. Mernissi, *Women and Islam*, 154–59.

53. Ibn Sa'd, *Tabaqat*, 8:205.

54. Ibid.

55. Qur'an 4:34.

56. Ibn Sa'd, *Tabaqat*, 8:204.

57. Lings, *Muhammad*, 215–30; Watt, *Muhammad at Medina*, 36–58; Mernissi, *Women and Islam*, 168–70.

58. Ibn Ishaq, 677, in Guillaume, *Life of Muhammad*.

59. Qur'an 33:12.

60. Qur'an 33:10–11.

61. Ibn Ishaq, 683, in Guillaume, *Life of Muhammad*.

62. Ibid., 689.

63. Aslan, *No god but God*, 91–98; Norman A. Stillman, *The Jews of Arab Lands* (Philadelphia, 1979).

64. Qur'an 29:46, Asad translation.

5. *Salam*

1. Muhammad ibn 'Umar al-Waqidi, *Kitab al-Maghazi*, 488–490, in Martin Lings, *Muhammad: His Life Based on the Earliest Sources* (London, 1983), 227.

2. Fatima Mernissi, *Women and Islam: An Historical and Theological Enquiry*, trans. Mary Jo Lakeland (Oxford, 1991), 17–172.

3. Qur'an 33:51, 63.

4. Qur'an 33:59–60.

5. Lings, *Muhammad*, 212–214; Tor Andrae, *Muhammad: The*

Man and His Faith, trans. Theophil Menzil (London, 1936), 215–16.

6. Qur'an 33:36–40.

7. Qur'an 33:53, in Muhammad Asad, trans., *The Message of the Qur'an* (Gibraltar, 1980).

8. Qur'an 33:53, 59.

9. Mernissi, *Women and Islam,* 88–191; Leila Ahmed, *Women and Gender in Islam* (New Haven and London, 1992), 53–57.

10. Mernissi, *Women and Islam,* 177–78; Lings, *Muhammad,* 235–45; W. Montgomery Watt, *Muhammad at Medina* (Oxford, 1956), 185–86; Ahmed, *Women and Gender in Islam,* 51.

11. Muhammad Ibn Ishaq, *Sirat Rasul Allah,* 726, in A. Guillaume, trans. and ed., *The Life of Muhammad: A Translation of Ishaq's* Sirat Rasul Allah (London, 1955).

12. Qur'an 12:18, Asad translation.

13. Ibn Ishaq, *Sirat Rasul Allah,* 735, in Guillaume, *Life of Muhammad.*

14. Qur'an 24:11.

15. Lings, *Muhammad,* 247–55; Andrae, *Muhammad,* 219–27; Watt, *Muhammad at Medina,* 46–59, 234–35; Mohammad A. Bamyeh, *The Social Origins of Islam, Mind, Economy, Discourse* (Minneapolis, 1999), 222–27.

16. Ibn Ishaq, *Sirat Rasul Allah,* 748, in Guillaume, *Life of Muhammad.*

17. Ibid., 741.

18. Ibid., 743.

19. Ibid.

20. Ibid., 745.

21. Watt, *Muhammad at Medina,* 50.

22. Qur'an 2:193.

23. Ibn Ishaq, *Sirat Rasul Allah,* 748, in Guillaume, *Life of Muhammad.*

24. Ibid., 747.

25. Bamyeh, *Social Origins of Islam,* 226–27.

26. Mernissi, *Women in Islam,* 184–86.

27. Ibn Ishaq, *Sirat Rasul Allah,* 747, in Guillaume, *Life of Muhammad.*

28. Ibid., 748.

29. Lings, *Muhammad,* 254.

30. Ibid., 255.

31. Qur'an 48:26, translation by Toshihiko Izutsu, *Ethico-Religious Concepts in the Qur'an* (Montreal and Kingston, ON, 2002), 31.

32. Qur'an 48:29, in Arthur J. Arberry, *The Koran Interpreted* (Oxford, 1964).

33. Ibn Ishaq, *Sirat Rasul Allah,* 751, in Guillaume, *Life of Muhammad.*

34. Qur'an 110, in Michael Sells, ed. and trans., *Approaching the Qur'an, The Early Revelations* (Ashland, OR, 1999).

35. Ibn Sa'd, *Kitab al-Tabaqat al-Kabir,* 7:147, in Lings, *Muhammad,* 271.

36. Lings, *Muhammad,* 282.

37. Ibn Ishaq, *Sirat Rasul Allah*, 717, in Guillaume, *Life of Muhammad*.

38. Qur'an 17:82, Arberry translation.

39. Ibn Ishaq, *Sirat Rasul Allah*, 821, in Asad, *Message of the Qur'an*, 794.

40. Qur'an 49:13, Asad translation.

41. Abu Ja'far at-Tabari, *Tariq ar-Rasul wa'-Muluk*, 1642, in Guillaume, *Life of Muhammad*, 553.

42. Lings, *Muhammad*, 311.

43. Ibn Ishaq, *Sirat Rasul Allah*, 886, in Guillaume, *Life of Muhammad*.

44. Bamyeh, *Social Origins of Islam*, 227–29.

45. Waqidi, 837–38, in Bamyeh, *Social Origins of Islam*, 228.

46. Ibn Ishaq, *Sirat Rasul Allah*, 969, in Guillaume, *Life of Muhammad*.

47. Ibid., 1006.

48. Ibid., 1006.

49. Ibid., 1012.

50. Qur'an 3:144, Arberry translation.

51. Ibn Ishaq, *Sirat Rasul Allah*, 1013, in Guillaume, *Life of Muhammad*.

52. Wilfred Cantwell Smith, *Islam in Modern History* (Princeton and London, 1957), 305.